# Malta Travel Guide 2023

"Exploring Malta: The Ultimate Travel Guide to a Mediterranean Gem"

## James S. Abbott

All rights reserved. No part of this publication may be reproduced, distributed, or transmitted in any form or by any means, including photocopying, recording, or other electronic or mechanical methods, without the prior written permission of the publisher, except in the case of brief quotations embodied in critical reviews and certain other noncommercial uses permitted by copyright law.

**Copyright © James S. Abbott, 2023**

# Table of Content

## Chapter 1
**Introduction to Malta**
- Brief overview of Malta's geography, history, and cultural significance
- Introduce the purpose of the travel guide and how it will help readers plan their trip effectively

## Chapter 2
**Getting to Know Malta**
- Overview of Malta's main islands: Malta, Gozo, and Comino
- Climate and best time to visit
- Visa requirements and travel essentials
- Transportation options and getting around the islands

## Chapter 3
**Exploring Valletta, the Capital City**
- Detailed description of Valletta's historical sites, including St. John's Co-Cathedral,

Grandmaster's Palace, and Upper Barrakka Gardens
- Recommendations for walking tours and exploring the city's narrow streets and charming squares
- Insider tips for experiencing Valletta's vibrant cultural scene and local cuisine

## Chapter 4
## Discovering Mdina and Rabat
- Highlights of the ancient walled city of Mdina and neighboring Rabat
- Must-visit attractions, such as St. Paul's Cathedral and the Mdina Dungeons
- Recommendations for enjoying a peaceful stroll through Mdina's picturesque streets and exploring Rabat's hidden gems

## Chapter 5
## Unveiling the Beauty of Gozo
- Introduction to Gozo's tranquil atmosphere and natural beauty

- Iconic sites like the Azure Window (formerly), Victoria's Citadel, and the Ggantija Temples
- Outdoor activities, including hiking, diving, and exploring Gozo's charming villages and stunning coastal areas

## Chapter 6
## Relaxing in Comino and the Blue Lagoon
- Detailed guide to the small island of Comino and its renowned Blue Lagoon
- Tips for enjoying the crystal-clear waters, sunbathing on pristine beaches, and snorkeling in vibrant marine life
- Insight into Comino's peaceful ambiance and opportunities for nature walks

## Chapter 7
## Delving into Malta's History and Culture
- Exploration of Malta's ancient temples, such as Hagar Qim and Mnajdra

- Overview of the Knights of St. John and their influence on the islands
- Recommendations for attending cultural events, and festivals, and experiencing local traditions

## Chapter 8
## Outdoor Adventures in Malta
- Exciting water sports activities, including scuba diving, snorkeling, and sailing
- Suggestions for hiking and cycling routes, with descriptions of scenic trails
- Thrilling experiences like cliff jumping, rock climbing, and horseback riding

## Chapter 9
## Savory Delights: Maltese Cuisine
- Introduction to Maltese cuisine and its Mediterranean influences
- Must-try dishes and local specialties, such as pastizzi, fenkata (rabbit stew), and ftira (traditional Maltese bread)

- Recommendations for restaurants, food markets, and culinary experiences across the islands

## Chapter 10
## Practical Information and Tips
- Essential travel information, including currency, language, and safety tips
- Suggestions for accommodations, from luxury resorts to budget-friendly options
- Local customs, etiquette, and useful phrases to enhance the travel experience

## Conclusion:
- Recap of the unique experiences and attractions Malta offers
- Encouragement for readers to plan their adventure and create lasting memories in this captivating Mediterranean destination

# Chapter 1

## Introduction to Malta

A Comprehensive Exploration of Geography, History, and Cultural Significance

Welcome to the captivating archipelago of Malta, where history comes alive amidst stunning natural landscapes. In this comprehensive overview, we will delve into the intricate tapestry of Malta's geography, delve deeper into its intriguing history, and explore the vibrant cultural significance that makes it a truly unique and compelling destination.

Geography: An Island Paradise

Malta's geography is a captivating blend of diverse landscapes and natural wonders. Three main islands make up the archipelago, which is situated in the middle Mediterranean Sea: Malta, Gozo, and Comino. . The islands are blessed with a Mediterranean climate, boasting mild winters and hot summers, making it an ideal year-round destination for travelers.

The larger island of Malta, home to the bustling capital city of Valletta, showcases a rich tapestry of geographic features. From its rocky cliffs and hidden coves to its golden sandy beaches, Malta offers an array of coastal beauty. Inland, rolling hills and fertile plains adorned with vineyards and olive groves paint a picturesque backdrop.

Gozo, the smaller sister island, offers a more serene and rural atmosphere. With its charming villages, rugged coastlines, and idyllic countryside, Gozo is a haven for nature lovers and those seeking tranquility.

Comino, the smallest and least inhabited island, boasts a breathtaking beauty. Its crown jewel, the Blue Lagoon, is renowned for its crystal-clear turquoise waters, making it a must-visit destination for snorkeling, swimming, and sunbathing.

Historical Tapestry: Unraveling the Past

Malta's history stretches back thousands of years, and each era has left its mark on the island's cultural heritage. Let's journey through the significant chapters of Malta's captivating history.

Prehistoric Era: Malta's prehistoric era is a testament to the island's ancient roots. The megalithic temples, including Ħaġar Qim, Mnajdra, and Tarxien, stand as remarkable achievements of the Neolithic period, predating even the Egyptian pyramids. These UNESCO World Heritage sites
provide a glimpse into the lives and beliefs of Malta's earliest inhabitants.

Phoenician and Roman Periods: In the 8th century BCE, Phoenician traders established a settlement on Malta, leaving their indelible mark on the islands' cultural fabric. The Roman period followed, bringing advancements in infrastructure, including the construction of roads, villas, and public buildings.

Arab and Norman Rule: The Arab era, which began in 870 CE, introduced Islamic influences that shaped Malta's language, architecture, and cuisine. The Normans conquered Malta in 1091, bringing a period of Christian influence that left lasting imprints on the islands' religious and cultural practices.

Knights of St. John: One of the most significant chapters in Malta's history unfolded with the arrival of the Knights Hospitaller, later known as the Knights of St. John, in 1530. They transformed Malta into a formidable fortress against Ottoman invasions, fortifying the islands with magnificent bastions, towers, and fortresses. The capital city of Valletta, a UNESCO World Heritage site, was meticulously planned and constructed during this period, showcasing the Knights' architectural prowess.

French and British Rule: In 1798, Napoleon Bonaparte briefly occupied Malta before the islands
fell under British control in 1800. British rule brought advancements in education, infrastructure, and governance, leaving an indelible impact on the islands. Malta attained independence in 1964, established a republican government in 1974, and ascended to EU membership in 2004.

## Cultural Significance: An Enchanting Melting Pot

Malta's cultural significance lies in its rich tapestry of traditions, art, and cuisine. The Maltese people are proud of their heritage and have preserved their customs and practices throughout the centuries.

Festivals and Religious Celebrations: Festas, dedicated to patron saints, are at the heart of Maltese culture. These vibrant religious festivals feature colorful processions, traditional music, fireworks, and ornate decorations adorning the streets. The Feast of St. Paul's Shipwreck in Valletta and the Santa Marija Feast in Gozo are among the most renowned celebrations.

Artistic Expressions: Malta's artistic heritage is diverse and vibrant. From traditional crafts such as filigree jewelry and delicate lacework to contemporary art exhibitions and open-air performances, creativity flourishes on the islands. The vibrant arts scene is showcased in galleries, theaters, and street performances throughout the year.

Architectural Marvels: Malta's architectural heritage is a testament to its rich history. The islands are adorned with splendid examples of Baroque, Gothic, and Renaissance architecture. Magnificent churches, palaces, and public squares in Valletta, Mdina, and other towns bear witness to the island's illustrious past.

Culinary Delights: Maltese cuisine is a delightful fusion of Mediterranean flavors, reflecting the islands' cultural influences throughout his**tory**. Traditional dishes like rabbit stew (fenkata), pastizzi (savory pastries), and ftira (local bread) tantalize the taste buds. Fresh seafood, sun-ripened tomatoes, and locally produced wines add to the culinary allure of the islands.

Malta's captivating geography, storied history, and vibrant cultural significance make it a truly remarkable destination. From exploring ancient temples to basking in the natural beauty of its coastlines, visitors are immersed in a journey through time. The cultural tapestry woven by various civilizations has left an indelible mark on the islands' traditions, architecture, and cuisine. Whether strolling through Valletta's charming streets, meandering along Gozo's tranquil paths, or discovering the hidden gems of Comino, Malta promises a captivating adventure for every traveler seeking to uncover its secrets.

Purpose of the Travel Guide:

The purpose of this travel guide is to empower you, the reader, with comprehensive information and resources to plan your trip to Malta effectively. By equipping you with essential knowledge and insights, we aim to enhance your understanding of the destination, allowing you to make informed decisions and create a personalized itinerary that suits your interests, preferences, and available time.

How This Guide Will Help You:
1. Destination Overview:
We will provide you with a detailed overview of Malta's geography, history, and cultural significance. Understanding the background of the destination will enable you to appreciate its unique character and context, enhancing your overall travel experience.

2. Planning Your Visit:
We will guide you through the practical aspects of planning your trip, including the best time to visit Malta based on climate, festivals, and crowd levels. By offering insights into different seasons and their advantages, we help you choose the optimal time for your visit, whether you prefer mild weather, vibrant cultural celebrations, or quieter periods.

3. Getting to Know Malta:
Navigating the Maltese islands can be overwhelming without proper guidance. We will provide you with information on how to reach Malta, including flight options to Malta International Airport (MLA) and ferry connections from neighboring regions. We will also discuss transportation options within Malta, such as public buses, taxis, and car rentals, enabling you to select the most convenient and cost-effective mode of transportation for your needs.

4. Exploring the Highlights:
Our guide will showcase the must-visit attractions of Malta, Gozo, and Comino, the three main islands that comprise the archipelago. We will provide in-depth descriptions and historical background for each site, including Valletta, Mdina, Gozo's natural wonders, and the iconic Blue Lagoon. Additionally, we will offer suggested itineraries, maps, and walking

routes to help you optimize your time and make the most of your visit.

5. Immersing in Culture and History:
Malta is steeped in a rich tapestry of history and culture, and we will guide you through its fascinating heritage. From exploring ancient temples, such as Hagar Qim and Mnajdra, to uncovering the legacy of the Knights of St. John, we will provide insights into the remarkable historical sites, museums, and traditions that make Malta a treasure trove for history enthusiasts.

6. Outdoor Adventures and Recreational Activities:
For nature lovers and adventure seekers, Malta offers a diverse range of outdoor activities. We will introduce you to thrilling experiences like scuba diving, snorkeling, hiking, and cycling. Our guide will highlight the best spots for these activities, ensuring you have an exhilarating and memorable journey through Malta's natural landscapes.

7. Culinary Delights:

Food is an integral part of any travel experience, and Malta's cuisine is a delightful fusion of Mediterranean flavors. We will introduce you to the unique dishes and local specialties, recommend traditional restaurants and markets, and provide insights into the Maltese culinary scene. From savoring pastizzi (traditional pastries) to indulging in a hearty fenkata (rabbit stew), you will embark on a gastronomic adventure that showcases the island's distinct flavors.

By using this travel guide, you will have the tools and knowledge to plan a remarkable journey to Malta. We aim to simplify the process, allowing you to navigate the destination with confidence, make informed decisions, and create an itinerary that suits your interests and preferences. Get ready to immerse yourself in Malta's rich history, stunning landscapes, vibrant culture, and delectable cuisine. Let "Discover Malta" be your trusted companion as you uncover the secrets of this enchanting Mediterranean gem. Safe travels!

# Chapter 2
## Getting to Know Malta

Malta, a beautiful Mediterranean archipelago, consists of three main islands: Malta, Gozo, and Comino. In this chapter, we will explore the best ways to reach Malta, the ideal time to visit, and the essential information to ensure a smooth journey.

1. Getting to Malta:
Malta is well-connected to major cities in Europe and other continents, making it easily accessible by air and sea.

- By Air: Malta International Airport (MLA) is the main gateway to the islands. It offers numerous direct flights from various European cities, as well as connecting flights from other parts of the world. Major airlines such as Air Malta, Ryanair, and EasyJet operate regular flights to Malta.

- By Sea: If you prefer a scenic journey, you can reach Malta by ferry or cruise ship. Ferries operate between Malta and neighboring Sicily, Italy, providing an opportunity to enjoy the picturesque Mediterranean views.

2. Best Time to Visit:
To make the most of your trip to Malta, it's important to consider the weather, crowd levels, and specific events or festivals happening during different seasons. The following are the best times to visit:

- Spring (April to June): This is considered the ideal time to visit Malta. The weather is nice, with comfortable highs of 15°C to 25°C (59°F to 77°F). The springtime blooms add charm to the landscapes, and the tourist crowds are relatively thin compared to the peak summer season.

- Autumn (September to October): Another favorable time to visit Malta is during the autumn months. The weather remains warm, with temperatures ranging from 20°C to 28°C (68°F to 82°F). It's a great time to enjoy outdoor activities, explore historical sites, and attend cultural events.

- Summer (July to August): While summer brings hot and dry weather, with temperatures reaching up to 35°C (95°F), it is the peak tourist season in Malta. The beaches are bustling, and the islands come alive with festivals and vibrant nightlife. If you don't mind the heat and crowds, this is the time to soak up the Mediterranean sun.

- Winter (November to February): Malta experiences mild winters, with temperatures ranging from 10°C to 18°C (50°F to 64°F). Although it's the offseason, winter can be a great time to visit for those seeking a quieter and more affordable experience. Some attractions may have limited hours or be closed, but you can still enjoy cultural activities and explore indoor sites.

3. Visa Requirements and Travel Essentials: Before traveling to Malta, it's essential to check visa requirements based on your country of origin. Here are some essential ideas to bear in mind:

- Visa-exempt countries: Citizens of the European Union (EU), the United States, Canada, Australia, and many other countries do not require a visa for short visits (up to 90 days). However, it's always best to check the latest visa regulations before your trip.

- Valid Passport: Ensure your passport is valid for at least six months beyond your intended stay in Malta.

- Travel Insurance: It is highly recommended to have travel insurance that covers medical expenses, trip cancellations, and any unforeseen emergencies.

- Health and Safety: Malta has a high standard of healthcare, but it's advisable to have travel insurance that covers medical evacuation if needed. It's also recommended to be up-to-date on routine vaccinations.

4. Transportation Options and Getting Around:
Once you arrive in Malta, you'll find several transportation options to explore the islands.

- Public Transportation: Malta has a reliable bus network operated by Malta Public Transport. Buses connect major towns, tourist sites, and the airport. You can purchase tickets onboard or opt for a reloadable Tallinja card for discounted fares.

- Taxis: Taxis are readily available, and you can find them at designated taxi stands or book them through a taxi service. It's advisable to check the rates beforehand and ensure the driver uses the meter.

- Car Rental: Renting a car is a popular option for travelers who want more freedom and flexibility. You'll find numerous car rental companies at the airport and in major towns. Remember to drive on the left side of the road in Malta.

- Ferries: If you plan to visit Gozo or Comino, you can take a ferry from Cirkewwa (in the north of Malta) to Mgarr (in Gozo) or Comino. The ferry service is operated by Gozo Channel.

5. Maps, Itineraries, and Suggested Routes: To make the most of your time in Malta, it's helpful to have maps, suggested itineraries, and routes to guide your exploration. Here are a few recommendations:

- Valletta: Start your journey in the capital city of Valletta. Take a guided walking tour to discover its historical sites, such as The Grandmaster's Palace, the Upper Barrakka Gardens, and St. John's Co-Cathedral. Enjoy a stroll along Republic Street, exploring the shops, cafes, and museums.

- Mdina and Rabat: Visit the medieval town of Mdina, known as the "Silent City." Explore its narrow streets, admire the architecture, and visit attractions like St. Paul's Cathedral and the Mdina Dungeons. Afterward, head to neighboring Rabat to explore the catacombs, Roman Villa, and the beautiful Domus Romana.

- Gozo: Plan a day trip or spend a couple of days on the tranquil island of Gozo. Explore Victoria, the capital, and visit the Citadel, which offers panoramic views of the island. Discover the natural wonders, including the Azure Window (formerly), Ramla Bay, and the fascinating Ggantija Temples.

- Comino and the Blue Lagoon: Take a boat trip to Comino and spend a relaxing day at the famous Blue Lagoon. Enjoy swimming in the crystal-clear waters and sunbathing on the pristine sandy beach. Take a walk around the island to appreciate its untouched beauty and peaceful atmosphere.

- Historical Sites and Temples: Don't miss the ancient temples of Hagar Qim and Mnajdra, which are UNESCO World Heritage sites. Explore the intricate stone structures and learn about Malta's prehistoric past.

By utilizing maps and following suggested itineraries, you can efficiently navigate Malta's attractions and make the most of your time on the islands.

Remember to plan your trip, consider the best time to visit based on your preferences, and have all the necessary travel essentials to ensure a memorable and hassle-free experience in Malta.

# Chapter 3

## Exploring Valletta, the Capital City

Valletta, the capital city of Malta, is a treasure trove of historical landmarks, architectural marvels, and vibrant cultural experiences. Immerse yourself in the grandeur of this UNESCO World Heritage site as you stroll through its narrow streets and discover the secrets of its rich past.

1. Introduction to Valletta:
Valletta, often referred to as the "City of Knights," was founded by the Knights of St. John in the 16th century. This fortified city is renowned for its well-preserved Baroque

architecture, majestic palaces, and charming squares.

2. St. John's Co-Cathedral:
A visit to Valletta is incomplete without stepping inside the magnificent St. John's Co-Cathedral. Marvel at its ornate interior, adorned with intricate marble work, gilded decorations, and masterful paintings by renowned artists such as Caravaggio. Take your time to admire the famous Beheading of St. John the Baptist and the remarkable floor made up of tombstones memorializing the knights.

3. Grandmaster's Palace:
Explore the opulent Grandmaster's Palace, which served as the official residence of the Grand Master of the Knights of St. John. Wander through its lavish State Rooms, adorned with tapestries, armor, and historic artifacts. Don't miss the stunning frescoes in the Council Chamber and the Armory,

displaying an impressive collection of weaponry.

**4. Upper Barrakka Gardens:**
Indulge in panoramic views of the Grand Harbor and the Three Cities from the serene Upper Barrakka Gardens. This beautifully landscaped public garden offers a tranquil escape from the bustling streets of Valletta. Take a stroll, relax on one of the benches, and soak in the breathtaking vistas.

**5. Exploring Valletta's Streets and Squares:**
Valletta's charm lies in its narrow streets, lined with colorful balconies and facades. Wander through Merchant Street, the main shopping thoroughfare, where you'll find a mix of local shops, international brands, and traditional Maltese craft stores. Discover hidden gems like Strait Street, once known as "The Gut" and a hub for nightlife in the past.

6. Suggested Walking Tour:
Embark on a self-guided walking tour to fully appreciate Valletta's beauty and history. Start at City Gate and proceed to St. John's Co-Cathedral. From there, head to the Grandmaster's Palace and continue towards the Lower Barrakka Gardens, offering more captivating views of the harbor. End your tour at Fort St. Elmo, where you can explore the National War Museum and learn about Malta's military history.

7. Map of Valletta:
Included in this chapter is a detailed map of Valletta, highlighting key attractions, recommended walking routes, and points of interest. Use this map to navigate the city and make the most of your time in Valletta.

8. Cultural Experiences in Valletta:
Valletta is a hub of cultural activities, offering a variety of experiences that showcase the vibrant arts scene and local

traditions. Visit the National Museum of Archaeology to learn about Malta's prehistoric past and see ancient artifacts. Explore the contemporary art exhibitions at the MUŻA, Malta's flagship art museum located in a historic building. Don't miss the opportunity to catch a performance at the Manoel Theatre, one of the oldest working theaters in Europe.

9. Dining in Valletta:
Valletta boasts a diverse culinary scene, ranging from traditional Maltese cuisine to international flavors. Sample local delicacies such as pastizzi (flaky pastries filled with ricotta or peas), rabbit stew (fenkata), and fresh seafood. Stroll through Strait Street, which has transformed into a trendy hub of restaurants, bars, and cafes offering a mix of local and international cuisine.

10. Shopping in Valletta:
Valletta offers a range of shopping experiences, from designer boutiques to

traditional craft stores. Explore the pedestrian-friendly Republic Street, lined with local shops selling handmade ceramics, silverware, and artisanal products. Visit the open-air market, Marsaxlokk, known for its fresh seafood and vibrant atmosphere, to purchase local delicacies and souvenirs.

11. Valletta's Festivals and Events:
Valletta hosts a variety of festivals and events throughout the year, celebrating music, art, and culture. The Valletta Baroque Festival, held in January, showcases the city's rich Baroque heritage through music performances and visual arts. The Malta International Arts Festival, taking place in summer, features a diverse program of theater, dance, music, and visual arts. Plan your visit accordingly to coincide with these events for an immersive cultural experience.

12. Practical Tips for Visiting Valletta:
- Consider purchasing the Valletta City Card, which offers discounted access to various attractions and public transportation within the city.
- Wear comfortable walking shoes, as Valletta's streets are hilly and paved with uneven stones.
- Take advantage of the numerous guided tours available to gain deeper insights into Valletta's history and hidden gems.
- Plan your visit during the early morning or late afternoon to avoid the crowds, especially during peak tourist season.

13. Nearby Attractions:
While exploring Valletta, you can also venture to nearby attractions that are within easy reach of the city. Just a short ferry ride away, you can visit the historical Three Cities—Vittoriosa, Senglea, and Cospicua—each boasting its own unique charm and architectural wonders. Discover the ancient forts, quaint marinas, and

charming waterfront promenades that tell stories of Malta's maritime history.

14. Staying in Valletta:
Valletta offers a range of accommodation options to suit different budgets and preferences. From luxury boutique hotels to cozy guesthouses and self-catering apartments, you can find a place to stay within the city's walls or nearby. Consider staying in a heritage hotel to immerse yourself in the city's historical ambiance.

15. Valletta's Evening Atmosphere:
As the sun sets, Valletta transforms into a magical destination, with a lively evening atmosphere that captivates visitors. Enjoy a stroll along the waterfront promenade, lined with waterfront restaurants and cafes offering stunning views of the Grand Harbor. Experience the city's vibrant

nightlife scene, with bars and pubs hosting live music performances and cultural events.

16. Valletta Film Locations:
Valletta has served as a backdrop for numerous films and TV shows, thanks to its architectural beauty and unique atmosphere. Movie enthusiasts can explore the city and discover locations featured in productions such as "Gladiator," "Game of Thrones," and "Murder on the Orient Express." Engage in a film location tour or explore independently to unveil Valletta's cinematic secrets.

17. Valletta's Hidden Gems:
Valletta is full of hidden gems that are waiting to be discovered. Step into the quiet courtyards of the Auberge de Castille, one of the grandest palaces in Valletta, which now serves as the Prime Minister's Office. Visit the Malta Postal Museum, tucked away in a charming side street, to learn about the

island's postal history and view unique stamp collections.

18. Valletta's Green Spaces:
Despite being a bustling city, Valletta offers serene green spaces where you can unwind and enjoy nature. Apart from the Upper Barrakka Gardens, visit the Lower Barrakka Gardens, which are smaller but equally delightful, offering a peaceful oasis amidst the cityscape. These gardens are perfect for a relaxing picnic or a moment of tranquility amid your explorations.

19. Sustainable Travel in Valletta:
Valletta is committed to sustainability, and travelers can contribute to preserving the city's cultural and environmental heritage. Opt for eco-friendly activities and support local businesses that promote sustainable practices. Reduce waste by carrying a reusable water bottle and exploring the city on foot or using public transportation.

20. Valletta's Future:
Valletta continues to evolve and adapt while preserving its historical charm. The city is designated as the European Capital of Culture for 2022, showcasing its rich cultural heritage through a year-long program of events, exhibitions, and performances. Keep an eye on the city's future developments, such as the ongoing revitalization projects and the emergence of new cultural and artistic initiatives.

21. Valletta's Religious Heritage:
Valletta is home to various churches and religious sites that hold great significance. Visit the Church of St. Paul's Shipwreck, where the shipwreck of the Apostle Paul is believed to have occurred. Explore the Carmelite Church of Our Lady of Mount Carmel, known for its stunning architecture and religious relics. Don't miss the Basilica of Our Lady of Mount Carmel, a magnificent church that hosts the annual Feast of St.

Paul's Shipwreck, a grand celebration of Maltese culture and faith.

## 22. Maritime Heritage:

Valletta's location on the Grand Harbor has shaped its rich maritime history. Visit the Malta Maritime Museum to learn about the island's seafaring traditions, naval history, and the role of the Knights of St. John in protecting the Mediterranean. Take a boat tour or harbor cruise to experience the city from a different perspective and appreciate its strategic importance throughout history.

## 23. Valletta Waterfront:

Experience the vibrant atmosphere of the Valletta Waterfront, a lively promenade lined with restaurants, cafes, and shops housed in historic warehouses. Enjoy a meal with waterfront views or indulge in some retail therapy while admiring the stunning views of the harbor. The Valletta Waterfront is a popular spot for both locals and visitors, especially during the evenings when it comes alive with entertainment and live performances.

24. Festivals and Events in Valletta:
Valletta hosts a range of festivals and events throughout the year, celebrating various aspects of Maltese culture. The Valletta Carnival, held in February, brings the streets to life with colorful costumes, parades, and festivities. The Valletta Green Festival, taking place in May, showcases sustainable practices, floral displays, and gardening workshops. Plan your visit accordingly to immerse yourself in the lively spirit of Valletta's festivals.

25. Valletta's Underground World:
Discover Valletta's hidden underground world through a visit to the Lascaris War Rooms. This secret underground complex was a strategic nerve center during World War II and offers a fascinating insight into Malta's wartime history. Explore the

intricate network of tunnels, operations rooms, and communication centers that played a crucial role in the defense of the island.

26. Boutique Shopping in Valletta:
Valletta is known for its boutique shopping scene, offering a unique selection of locally designed fashion, handmade crafts, and artisanal products. Explore the side streets and alleyways to discover independent boutiques, art galleries, and concept stores. Support local designers and artisans by purchasing one-of-a-kind souvenirs, jewelry, or clothing that reflects the authentic spirit of Malta.

27. Valletta's Nightlife:
Valletta comes alive after dark with a vibrant nightlife scene catering to various tastes. Enjoy live music performances at intimate jazz bars or rooftop venues offering panoramic views of the city. Explore trendy wine bars and craft beer pubs that showcase

local and international beverages. Experience the vibrant energy of Valletta's nightlife as you mingle with locals and fellow travelers.

28. Valletta's Restoration Projects:
Valletta is an ever-evolving city, with ongoing restoration projects that aim to preserve and revitalize its architectural heritage. Stay updated on the restoration efforts of iconic landmarks such as the Royal Opera House, which was destroyed during World War II and is undergoing reconstruction. Witness the transformation of historical buildings and public spaces as Valletta strives to maintain its cultural significance.

29. Valletta's Gardens and Green Spaces:
Valletta may be a city, but it also offers pockets of lush greenery and tranquil gardens for relaxation and rejuvenation. Visit the Lower Barrakka Gardens, located near the waterfront, and revel in the

beautifully landscaped terraced gardens offering stunning views of the harbor. Admire the colorful flowers, statues, and fountains as you bask in the peaceful atmosphere. Additionally, the Hastings Gardens, situated on the bastions of Valletta, provide another serene oasis with its well-maintained pathways, shaded seating areas, and panoramic vistas.

30. Exploring Valletta's Neighborhoods:
Beyond the main attractions, Valletta is composed of distinct neighborhoods, each with its character and charm. Visit the residential area of Floriana, just outside the city walls, and enjoy its quaint streets and the stunning Argotti Botanic Gardens. Explore the bustling market town of Marsa, known for its vibrant local culture and fresh produce markets. Take time to wander through these lesser-known neighborhoods to gain a deeper appreciation for the local way of life.

31. Valletta's Hidden Cafes and Bakeries:
Valletta is home to numerous hidden cafes and bakeries, perfect for indulging in a delightful break during your exploration. Discover charming local establishments serving traditional Maltese pastries, such as the popular pastizzi or imqaimarette pastries). Unwind with a cup of locally roasted coffee or enjoy a leisurely afternoon tea accompanied by delectable cakes and sweets. These hidden gems offer an opportunity to savor the flavors of Malta while immersing yourself in the local café culture.

32. Artistic Heritage in Valletta:
Valletta has long been a hub for artists and creatives, fostering a vibrant artistic heritage. Explore the city's art scene by visiting contemporary art galleries and studios showcasing the works of local and international artists. The Valletta Contemporary, located in a converted warehouse, is a prominent space for

contemporary art exhibitions and cultural events. Immerse yourself in Valletta's creative atmosphere and discover the talent that thrives within its walls.

33. Valletta's Sustainable Initiatives:
Valletta is committed to sustainable practices and initiatives, aiming to preserve its cultural and environmental heritage. Numerous eco-friendly projects and organizations have emerged, promoting responsible tourism and environmental conservation. Engage in eco-tours, where knowledgeable guides educate visitors about Valletta's natural ecosystems and biodiversity. Support local businesses that prioritize sustainability, from eco-friendly accommodations to organic dining options. By embracing these initiatives, you can contribute to the long-term preservation of Valletta's beauty and sustainability.

34. Valletta's Modern Architecture:
While Valletta is renowned for its Baroque and medieval architecture, it also boasts modern structures that blend seamlessly with the city's historical fabric. Explore the striking contemporary architecture, such as the Parliament Building designed by renowned architect Renzo Piano. Marvel at the City Gate and the Triton Fountain, which underwent contemporary redesigns, creating a dialogue between the old and the new. Appreciate the harmonious coexistence of modern design and historical heritage within the city's streets.

35. Valletta's Sunset Views:
Witness the breathtaking beauty of Valletta at sunset, as the city's golden hues are cast upon its ancient walls. Find the perfect spot to enjoy the panoramic vistas of the sun sinking into the Mediterranean Sea. From the Upper Barrakka Gardens or the Valletta Waterfront, embrace the awe-inspiring

views and capture the magical moments as Valletta bids farewell to the day.

36. Valletta's Literary Connections:
Valletta has inspired many renowned authors and serves as the setting for various literary works. Dive into the literary world by exploring locations mentioned in books and novels set in Valletta. Walk in the footsteps of writers like Walter Scott and Patrick O'Brian, who drew inspiration from the city's rich history and unique atmosphere. Visit bookstores and libraries that offer a curated selection of Maltese literature, allowing you to delve deeper into the literary heritage of Valletta.

37. Valletta's Street Art:
While Valletta is known for its historical architecture, it also embraces contemporary art forms, including street art. Explore the city's vibrant street art scene, with murals and graffiti adorning the walls of buildings. Take a street art tour to learn about the

stories behind the artworks and the artists who have contributed to Valletta's urban art landscape. Witness the intersection of tradition and modernity as Valletta embraces this dynamic form of artistic expression.

38. Valletta's Music Scene:
Valletta is a hub of musical creativity and hosts various events and performances throughout the year. Immerse yourself in the city's music scene by attending concerts and recitals held in historic venues, churches, and open-air spaces. Experience the enchantment of classical music, traditional Maltese folk music, or contemporary performances by local and international artists. Embrace the harmonious melodies that resonate through the streets of Valletta.

39. Valletta's Hidden Cellars:
Beneath the streets of Valletta lie hidden cellars, once used for storage and various

purposes. Some of these cellars have been repurposed into unique spaces, such as wine bars, galleries, or performance venues. Discover these underground gems as you descend into the depths of Valletta, experiencing the hidden stories and the atmospheric ambiance of these subterranean spaces.

40. Valletta's Religious Processions:
Religious processions play a significant role in Maltese culture, and Valletta hosts several throughout the year. Witness the grandeur of processions, where religious statues are carried through the streets accompanied by hymns and prayers. The Good Friday procession, known as the Procession of the Dead Christ, is particularly notable, with its solemn atmosphere and intricate decorations adorning the streets of Valletta.

41. Valletta's Photography Opportunities:
Valletta provides ample opportunities for photographers to capture its architectural beauty, vibrant street scenes, and mesmerizing landscapes. Capture the golden light as it bathes the city's facades during sunrise or sunset. Wander through the city's narrow alleys, capturing the interplay of light and shadow. From the bustling markets to the tranquil gardens, every corner of Valletta offers a visual feast for photography enthusiasts.

42. Valletta's Film Festivals:
Valletta is a hub for film enthusiasts, hosting renowned film festivals that celebrate local and international cinema. The Valletta Film Festival showcases a diverse selection of films, including premieres, documentaries, and retrospectives. Immerse yourself in the world of cinema as you attend screenings, participate in workshops, and engage with filmmakers and industry professionals.

Valletta's allure extends beyond its historical landmarks and cultural significance. The city offers enchanting gardens, hidden cafes, artistic endeavors, sustainable initiatives, and a blend of modernity and tradition. By exploring Valletta's diverse neighborhoods, savoring local culinary delights, and embracing its artistic and sustainable endeavors, you'll uncover the city's hidden treasures. Immerse yourself in the soul of Valletta and let its beauty captivate you as you create cherished memories in this extraordinary capital city.

# Chapter 4
## Discovering Mdina and Rabat

Welcome to the captivating ancient city of Mdina and its neighboring town, Rabat. Nestled in the heart of Malta, these historic gems offer a glimpse into the island's rich past and architectural splendor. In this chapter, we will delve into the intricate details of Mdina and Rabat, exploring their fascinating history, must-visit attractions, recommended walking routes, and hidden treasures.

1. Mdina: The Silent City

Mdina, also known as the "Silent City," is a fortified medieval town perched on a hilltop, offering panoramic views of the surrounding countryside. As you step into its narrow streets and ancient walls, you'll be transported back in time.

1.1 Historical Significance:

Mdina traces its origins back over 4,000 years, making it one of Europe's oldest inhabited cities. It served as the capital of Malta until the arrival of the Knights of St. John in the 16th century. The city's architecture reflects a blend of influences from various periods, including Phoenician, Roman, and Arab.

1.2 Attractions:

a. St. Paul's Cathedral: Admire the stunning Baroque architecture of St. Paul's Cathedral, built on the site where the Roman governor Publius met St. Paul after his shipwreck. Marvel at the intricate marble work, intricate frescoes, and stunning altarpiece.

b. Palazzo Falson Historic House Museum: Explore the Palazzo Falson, a medieval mansion-turned-museum that houses an impressive collection of antiques, artwork, and historical artifacts. Step into the past as you wander through the beautifully preserved rooms and courtyards.

c. Mdina Dungeons: Descend into the depths of the Mdina Dungeons, where you can discover the dark and mysterious side of the city's history through interactive exhibits and immersive storytelling.

d. Bastion Square: Enjoy breathtaking views from Bastion Square, one of the best spots to witness Malta's stunning landscapes. Take in the panoramic vistas of the surrounding countryside, the distant sea, and neighboring towns.

1.3 Walking Routes:
To fully immerse yourself in the charm of Mdina, we recommend the following walking routes:

a. Main Gate to St. Paul's Cathedral: Start your journey at the Main Gate and wander through the medieval streets, taking in the architectural wonders and quaint alleys. Arrive at St. Paul's Cathedral, where you can explore its grandeur and religious significance.

b. Mdina Ramparts Walk: Embark on a stroll along the fortified walls of Mdina, enjoying picturesque views of the Maltese countryside. As you walk the ramparts, you'll pass by bastions, gardens, and hidden corners that offer unique perspectives of the city.

2. Rabat: Exploring the Ancient Town

Adjacent to Mdina lies Rabat, a charming town that boasts a wealth of historical sites, religious monuments, and hidden gems. Explore Rabat's winding streets and uncover its treasures.

2.1 Historical Significance:
Rabat has roots dating back to Roman times, and its name derives from the Arabic

word for "suburb." Over the centuries, it has been home to different civilizations, including the Romans, Arabs, and Knights of St. John.

2.2 Attractions:
a. Catacombs of St. Paul and St. Agatha: Venture beneath the streets of Rabat to discover the fascinating catacombs, a labyrinth of underground chambers and passageways used as burial grounds during the Roman era. Admire the elaborate frescoes and historic graves.

b. Domus Romana: Explore the remains of a Roman townhouse at Domus Romana, where you can witness the opulent lifestyles of ancient Roman inhabitants. Admire the well-preserved mosaic floors and learn about the daily lives of the Roman elite.

c. Wignacourt Museum: Visit the Wignacourt Museum, housed in a 17th-century palace, and explore its impressive collection of religious art, including paintings, sculptures, and intricate silverware. Learn about Malta's religious heritage through the museum's exhibits.

2.3 Walking Routes:
To make the most of your time in Rabat, consider the following walking routes:

a. Roman Heritage Walk: Begin at the Catacombs of St. Paul and St. Agatha, then meander through the streets of Rabat, passing by Roman ruins and historical landmarks. Immerse yourself in the town's rich heritage and fascinating stories.

b. Sacred Sites Trail: Embark on a journey of spirituality as you visit Rabat's various religious sites, including churches, chapels, and monasteries. Explore the architectural beauty and delve into the religious traditions that have shaped the town.

2.4 Hidden Treasures:
While exploring Mdina and Rabat, keep an eye out for these hidden treasures that add a touch of magic to your visit:

a. Greek Gate: Discover the Greek Gate, an ancient entrance to Mdina that provides a glimpse into the city's past. Admire its intricate carvings and imagine the footsteps of ancient travelers who passed through its arches.

b. Mdina Glass: Visit the Mdina Glass factory and witness the artistry of local glassblowers as they create exquisite glassware using traditional techniques. Browse through the beautiful collections and perhaps take home a unique piece of Maltese craftsmanship.

c. St. Paul's Catacombs: Delve further into the underground mysteries of Rabat at St. Paul's Catacombs, a complex network of interconnected burial chambers. Explore the fascinating burial rituals and architectural features of this historical site.

d. Casa Bernard: Step into the elegant Casa Bernard, a palatial house that showcases the grandeur of Maltese aristocratic living. Admire the opulent interiors, including stunning frescoes and intricate decor, offering a glimpse into the lifestyle of Malta's elite.

3. Best Time to Visit:
To make the most of your visit to Mdina and Rabat, it's recommended to plan your trip during the spring (April to June) or autumn (September to October) seasons. During these times, the weather is pleasant, and the tourist crowds are relatively smaller compared to the peak summer season. You'll have the opportunity to explore the attractions comfortably and enjoy the charm of Mdina and Rabat without feeling overwhelmed.

It's worth noting that Mdina takes on an enchanting atmosphere during the evening hours when the streets are illuminated, creating a magical ambiance. Consider visiting during this time to experience the city's beauty in a different light.

4. Maps, Itineraries, and Suggested Routes:
To assist you in navigating Mdina and Rabat effortlessly, we have provided detailed maps, itineraries, and suggested routes. These resources will help you maximize your time and ensure you don't miss out on any significant attractions or hidden gems. You can find these maps at the end of this chapter or refer to the online resources mentioned in the book for downloadable versions.

The maps highlight key attractions, walking routes, and points of interest, allowing you to plan your visit accordingly. The itineraries suggest a logical sequence of exploration, taking into account the proximity of sites and the time required to fully appreciate each location. However, feel free to customize your itinerary based on your interests and the amount of time you have available.

By following the suggested routes and utilizing the provided maps, you'll have a seamless and rewarding experience while uncovering the historical treasures of Mdina and Rabat.

Mdina and Rabat offer an immersive journey into Malta's rich history, architectural beauty, and hidden wonders. With their ancient streets, well-preserved sites, and captivating stories, these towns transport you to a bygone era. Take your time to explore the enchanting streets of Mdina, visit its impressive cathedral, and admire the panoramic views from its ramparts. In Rabat, venture underground to discover catacombs, explore ancient Roman remnants, and immerse yourself in the town's sacred sites. With careful planning, an open mind, and the information provided in this chapter, you're sure to have a memorable experience in Mdina and Rabat, discovering the essence of Malta's cultural heritage.

By exploring both Mdina and Rabat, you will uncover the layers of history and culture that have shaped Malta throughout the centuries. Take your time to immerse yourself in the ambiance of these ancient towns, wandering their streets, and discovering their hidden corners. With their unique charm and historical significance, Mdina and Rabat are sure to leave an indelible impression on your Malta travel experience.

# Chapter 5
## Unveiling the Beauty of Gozo

Welcome to the enchanting island of Gozo, a tranquil haven known for its idyllic landscapes, rich history, and warm hospitality. In this chapter, we will delve into the captivating beauty of Gozo and explore its must-visit attractions, outdoor activities, and hidden gems. Get ready to embark on a memorable journey through this picturesque Mediterranean gem.

1. Discovering Victoria, the Island's Capital:
Victoria, also known as Rabat, serves as the bustling capital of Gozo. Start your exploration at the heart of Victoria, the Citadel. This ancient fortified city showcases a blend of medieval and Baroque architecture. Marvel at the panoramic views of the island from the citadel's bastions and explore its fascinating historical sites,

including the Cathedral of the Assumption and the Old Prison.

2. Iconic Landmarks and Historical Sites:
Gozo is adorned with an array of iconic landmarks and historical sites that reflect its rich cultural heritage. Don't miss the Ggantija Temples, a UNESCO World Heritage site and one of the world's oldest freestanding structures. These prehistoric temples provide a glimpse into Gozo's ancient past and are a testament to the island's significance.

3. Azure Window and Inland Sea (Dwejra):
Although the natural limestone arch known as the Azure Window sadly collapsed in 2017, the site remains a must-visit for its dramatic coastal scenery. The Inland Sea, a small lagoon connected to the Mediterranean Sea, offers a unique experience for boat trips and swimming. Explore the surrounding cliffs and caves,

and witness the stunning rock formations carved by nature.

4. Idyllic Beaches and Crystal-clear Waters:
Gozo boasts an abundance of pristine beaches and crystal-clear waters, perfect for relaxation and water activities. Ramla Bay, with its reddish-golden sand and turquoise waters, is a popular choice among visitors. Other notable beaches include the secluded San Blas Bay and the serene Mgarr ix-Xini, which offers picturesque views and a tranquil atmosphere.

5. Outdoor Adventures and Nature Trails:
Gozo's unspoiled landscapes provide the ideal setting for outdoor enthusiasts. Lace up your hiking boots and embark on scenic coastal trails, such as the Victoria to Marsalforn Walk, which offers breathtaking views of the coastline. The countryside is dotted with charming villages and rolling hills, inviting you to explore its hidden gems on foot or by bicycle.

6. Cultural Experiences and Festivals:
Immerse yourself in Gozo's vibrant cultural scene by attending one of the island's lively festivals. The Feast of Santa Marija, held in Victoria every August, is a spectacular celebration of music, fireworks, and traditional processions. Experience the local way of life by visiting quaint villages like Xaghra, known for its charming square and historical landmarks.

7. Gastronomic Delights:
Indulge in Gozo's culinary treasures, characterized by fresh and locally sourced ingredients. Sample traditional dishes like the Gozitan ftira, a delicious flatbread topped with local produce and cheese. Visit the bustling food markets to taste an array of authentic flavors and learn about Gozo's gastronomic heritage.

8. Practical Information and Tips:
- Getting to Gozo: Reach Gozo from Malta via a short ferry ride from Cirkewwa to Mgarr. Ferries run regularly, providing convenient access to the island.
- Transportation on Gozo: Public buses are the primary mode of transportation on the island, connecting various towns and attractions. Car rental services are also available for more flexibility.
- Accommodations: Gozo offers a range of accommodations, from luxury resorts to guesthouses and farmhouses. Pre-order your tickets, especially during the busiest travel times.
- Safety and Etiquette: Gozo is generally a safe destination, but it's always advisable to take standard precautions. During your stay, be mindful of the locals' cultures, customs, and natural surroundings.

9. Hidden Gems and Off-the-Beaten-Path:
Gozo is filled with hidden gems that are worth discovering. Explore the quaint village of Xlendi, nestled in a picturesque

bay, and enjoy its charming waterfront promenade lined with restaurants and cafes. Visit the Ta' Pinu Basilica, a revered pilgrimage site known for its miraculous stories and stunning architecture. Take a stroll through the Xwejni Salt Pans, where you can witness the traditional method of salt harvesting and enjoy panoramic views of the coastline.

10. Exploring Underwater Wonders:
Gozo is a paradise for diving enthusiasts, offering an array of underwater wonders to explore. Discover vibrant marine life, fascinating caves, and unique rock formations. The Blue Hole, a natural sinkhole surrounded by breathtaking cliffs, is a popular dive site known for its crystal-clear waters and abundance of marine species. Experienced divers can also explore the wreck of the MV Karwela, an artificial reef teeming with marine life.

11. Day Trips to Comino:
While exploring Gozo, take advantage of its proximity to the neighboring island of Comino. Embark on a day trip and discover the unspoiled beauty of this tiny island. Relax on the famous Blue Lagoon's pristine beaches, snorkel in its turquoise waters, or explore the island's walking trails and hidden coves. Comino offers a tranquil escape and a chance to unwind amidst nature's splendor.

12. Suggested Itineraries and Routes:
To make the most of your time on Gozo, here are a few suggested itineraries and routes:

- Historic and Cultural Trail:
  - Morning: Explore the Citadel in Victoria, visiting the Cathedral and the museums within the fortified walls.

- Afternoon: Visit the Ggantija Temples and discover the rich prehistoric heritage of Gozo.
  - Evening: Enjoy a stroll through the picturesque streets of Xaghra, stopping by the Xaghra Parish Church and the Ta' Kola Windmill.

- Nature and Beach Escapade:
  - Morning: Begin your day with a visit to the Azure Window (Dwejra), followed by a boat trip to the Inland Sea.
  - Afternoon: Relax and unwind at Ramla Bay, one of Gozo's most beautiful beaches, known for its red sand and clear waters.
  - Evening: Watch the sunset from the cliffs near San Blas Bay, immersing yourself in the tranquility of nature.

- Adventure and Outdoor Exploration:
  - Morning: Embark on a hiking adventure along the coastal trail from Marsalforn to Xwejni Bay, taking in the breathtaking views.

- Afternoon: Discover the stunning Wied il-Mielaħ Window, a hidden gem located near the village of Għarb.

- Evening: Enjoy a thrilling rock climbing experience at the cliffs of Mgarr ix-Xini or try horseback riding through Gozo's beautiful countryside.

Gozo is a captivating island that promises a multitude of experiences, from exploring historical landmarks to immersing oneself in nature's beauty. Whether you're seeking tranquility on secluded beaches, diving into vibrant underwater worlds, or delving into the island's rich culture, Gozo offers an array of opportunities for discovery. Create your adventure, following suggested itineraries or forging your path, and let Gozo's quiet charm leave an indelible mark on your travel memories.

# Chapter 6

# Relaxing in Comino and the Blue Lagoon

Comino, a small island located between Malta and Gozo, is a haven for those seeking tranquility and natural beauty. Its main attraction, the Blue Lagoon, is renowned for its crystal-clear turquoise waters and picturesque surroundings. In this chapter, we will delve into the details of Comino and provide you with everything you need to know to make the most of your visit.

1. Introduction to Comino:
Comino, the smallest inhabited island in the Maltese archipelago, spans just 3.5 square kilometers. With no cars and a population of only four residents, it offers a peaceful retreat from the bustling mainland. The island's unspoiled landscapes, including rugged cliffs, hidden coves, and

breathtaking views, make it a must-visit destination.

2. The Blue Lagoon:
The Blue Lagoon is undoubtedly the highlight of Comino. This natural wonder features shallow, translucent waters that exhibit mesmerizing shades of blue. Visitors are captivated by the lagoon's beauty and often spend hours swimming, snorkeling, or simply basking in the sun on the sandy beach. The lagoon's unique geology, with limestone formations and underwater caves, adds to its allure.

3. Exploring the Blue Lagoon:
To fully appreciate the Blue Lagoon, it's recommended to arrive early in the day or later in the afternoon to avoid the crowds. During peak season, the lagoon can get quite busy, so planning your visit accordingly is crucial. You can reach the Blue Lagoon by taking a ferry from either Malta or Gozo,

with several companies offering regular services.

4. Enjoying Water Activities:
Snorkeling and swimming in the clear waters of the Blue Lagoon are highly recommended. The lagoon is teeming with marine life, including colorful fish and vibrant underwater flora. Snorkeling gear is readily available for rent on the island, allowing you to explore the underwater world at your leisure.

5. Exploring Comino's Walking Trails:
Beyond the Blue Lagoon, Comino offers picturesque walking trails that allow you to discover the island's natural beauty. One popular route is the Santa Marija Tower Walk, which takes you to Santa Marija Bay and offers stunning coastal views. Another option is the Comino Circular Walk, a longer trail that showcases the island's diverse landscapes, including its rugged cliffs and hidden coves.

6. Santa Marija Tower:
The Santa Marija Tower, also known as Comino Tower, is a prominent landmark on the island. Built by the Knights of St. John in the 17th century, the tower served as a lookout point to protect against pirate attacks. Today, it stands as a testament to Comino's rich history. Visiting the tower provides an opportunity to admire its architecture and enjoy panoramic views of the surrounding area.

7. Staying on Comino:
While Comino is a small island, it offers accommodation options for those who wish to extend their stay and experience its tranquility for more than just a day trip. The only hotel on the island, the Comino Hotel & Bungalows, provides a peaceful retreat surrounded by nature.

8. Exploring the Nearby Caves:
Comino's coastline is dotted with numerous caves waiting to be explored. The Santa Marija Caves, located near Santa Marija Bay, are particularly popular. These sea caves offer a unique and adventurous experience for visitors. You can access them by renting a kayak or joining a boat tour.

9. Protecting Comino's Natural Beauty:
Comino is a protected nature reserve, and it is essential to respect the environment during your visit. Avoid leaving any waste behind and be mindful of the delicate ecosystem both on land and underwater. Help preserve Comino's natural beauty for future generations to enjoy.

10. Practical Tips and Recommendations:
- Pack sunscreen, a hat, and plenty of water, as shade is limited on the island.
- Consider bringing your snacks or a picnic lunch, as food options on Comino are limited.

- Check the ferry schedules in advance to plan your trip accordingly.
- If you're prone to seasickness, consider taking necessary precautions, as the ferry ride to Comino can be choppy during rough weather.

11. Exploring Other Beaches and Bays:
While the Blue Lagoon is the most famous attraction on Comino, the island is also home to other beautiful beaches and bays worth exploring. Santa Marija Bay, located near the Santa Marija Tower, offers a sandy beach and calm waters ideal for swimming and sunbathing. San Niklaw Bay is another serene spot with crystal-clear waters and a pebbly beach, perfect for those seeking a quieter atmosphere away from the crowds of the Blue Lagoon.

12. Diving and Snorkeling Adventures:
Comino is a popular destination for diving enthusiasts due to its clear waters and diverse marine life. Several diving centers

on the island offer guided dives, catering to both beginners and experienced divers. Discover vibrant coral reefs, underwater caves, and fascinating sea creatures as you explore the depths of the Mediterranean Sea. Snorkeling is also a fantastic option for those who want to observe the marine world without scuba diving.

13. Birdwatching on Comino:
Comino's unspoiled landscapes provide a haven for various bird species, making it a paradise for birdwatchers. The island's cliffs and scrubland attract migratory birds during the spring and autumn seasons. Keep an eye out for species such as kestrels, peregrine falcons, and yellow-legged gulls as you explore Comino's walking trails and coastal areas.

14. Suggested Itineraries for Comino:
To make the most of your time on Comino, consider the following suggested itineraries:

- Day Trip Itinerary:
   - Morning: Start your day early and catch one of the first ferries to Comino.
   - Explore the Blue Lagoon and enjoy swimming and snorkeling.
   - Afternoon: Take a leisurely walk along the coastal trails or visit the Santa Marija Tower for panoramic views.
   - Relax on one of the quieter beaches, such as Santa Marija Bay or San Niklaw Bay.
   - Evening: Depart from Comino and return to Malta or Gozo.

- Extended Stay Itinerary:
   - Day 1: Explore the Blue Lagoon and enjoy water activities.
   - Day 2: Discover the walking trails, visit the Santa Marija Tower, and explore the nearby caves.
   - Day 3: Spend a day birdwatching and enjoying the natural beauty of the island.

- Day 4: Relax on the beaches, indulge in a picnic, or book a diving or snorkeling excursion.

- Day 5: Depart from Comino, taking with you cherished memories of the island's tranquility and natural wonders.

15. Environmental Conservation:
As a visitor to Comino, it is essential to respect the island's fragile ecosystem. Follow these conservation tips to ensure the preservation of its natural beauty:

- Avoid littering and dispose of waste properly.
- Stay on designated paths and trails to protect the flora and fauna.
- Do not disturb wildlife or remove any natural resources from the island.
- Use reef-safe sunscreen to protect the marine environment.

By immersing yourself in the serene ambiance of Comino, exploring its hidden gems, and appreciating its natural wonders, you'll create cherished memories and experience the true essence of this tranquil island.

Comino, with its stunning Blue Lagoon and unspoiled landscapes, offers a serene escape in the heart of the Mediterranean. Whether you spend a day or a few days exploring its beauty, you'll be captivated by the crystal-clear waters, hidden bays, and peaceful atmosphere. Make sure to plan your visit accordingly, bring essential items, and respect the island's environment to ensure a memorable and responsible experience on Comino.

# Chapter 7

# Delving into Malta's History and Culture

Malta is a destination steeped in rich history and vibrant culture that spans thousands of years. In this chapter, we will delve into the fascinating historical sites, ancient temples, and the unique cultural experiences that Malta has to offer.

1. Ancient Temples: Hagar Qim and Mnajdra

Malta is home to some of the world's oldest free-standing structures, known as the Megalithic Temples. Among these, Hagar Qim and Mnajdra are two remarkable sites that provide a window into Malta's prehistoric past. Situated on the southern coast of Malta, these temples date back over 5,000 years, pre-dating even the Egyptian pyramids. Explore the impressive megaliths, intricate carvings, and stone altars that were once used for religious ceremonies. Detailed explanations of the temples' layout, purpose, and historical significance will bring these ancient structures to life.

2. The Knights of St. John and Valletta's Grandmaster's Palace

Malta has a captivating history linked to the Knights of St. John, also known as the Knights Hospitaller. Discover the remarkable story of this military order and its pivotal role in defending Malta against the Ottoman Empire. Explore Valletta's Grandmaster's Palace, a grand architectural gem that served as the seat of power for the Knights. Inside, you'll find opulent staterooms, a fascinating armory, and an art collection that showcases the order's legacy. Gain insights into the Knights' traditions, codes of chivalry, and their lasting impact on Maltese society.

3. Cultural Events and Festivals

Malta's cultural calendar is filled with vibrant events and festivals that celebrate the island's heritage. Highlighting some of the most significant celebrations, such as the Malta International Arts Festival and the Valletta Baroque Festival, immerse yourself in the local arts scene. Learn about the traditional Maltese folk festivals and the annual Carnival, a colorful and lively event that takes place in February. Experience the joyous atmosphere, parades, music, and intricate costumes that make these festivals truly unforgettable.

4. Exploring Local Traditions

To truly understand Malta's culture, it's essential to explore its unique traditions and customs. Dive into the world of Maltese craftsmanship by visiting artisan workshops and learning about traditional skills passed down through generations. Discover the art of filigree, pottery, lace-making, and glassblowing. Engage in hands-on experiences, such as joining a culinary workshop to learn how to prepare traditional Maltese dishes like rabbit stew (fenkata) or pastizzi, a delicious savory pastry.

5. Cultural Highlights in Valletta

Valletta, the capital city of Malta, is a UNESCO World Heritage site renowned for its architectural marvels and historical significance. Stroll through the atmospheric streets and visit St. John's Co-Cathedral, a Baroque masterpiece adorned with intricate frescoes and the works of renowned artist Caravaggio. Explore the Upper Barrakka Gardens, offering breathtaking views of the Grand Harbor and the Three Cities. Discover the National Museum of Archaeology, where you can learn about Malta's prehistoric past, and the National Museum of Fine Arts, housing an impressive collection of art spanning various periods.

6. Cultural Gems in Mdina and Rabat

Journey to the ancient city of Mdina, also known as the "Silent City," and its neighboring town of Rabat. Explore the narrow winding streets, adorned with medieval architecture and palaces, and visit St. Paul's Cathedral, an architectural marvel that boasts stunning frescoes and intricate stone carvings. Discover the fascinating history of Mdina's noble families by exploring the palazzos, and delve into the catacombs and underground passages that lie beneath the streets of Rabat.

7. Historical Gems: Tarxien Temples and Ggantija Temples

In addition to Hagar Qim and Mnajdra, Malta is home to other significant ancient temples that showcase the island's rich prehistoric heritage. The Tarxien Temples, located in the southeastern part of Malta, date back to 3600-2500 BCE and are a UNESCO World Heritage site. Explore the intricate stone carvings, altars, and statues that provide insights into the religious beliefs and rituals of the temple builders.

On the island of Gozo, take advantage of the opportunity to visit the awe-inspiring Ggantija Temples. Dating back to 3600-3200 BCE, these temples are among the oldest free-standing structures in the world. Marvel at the massive stone blocks that make up the temples' walls and learn about the archaeological discoveries made on-site. The Ggantija Temples offer a captivating glimpse into Malta's Neolithic past and the advanced architectural skills of its ancient inhabitants.

8. Living Heritage: Traditional Villages and Crafts

To experience Malta's living heritage, venture beyond the major cities and explore the charming traditional villages. Places like Zebbug, Qormi, and Birkirkara offer a glimpse into traditional Maltese life, with their narrow streets, old houses, and quaint squares. Take a leisurely walk through these villages, interact with the friendly locals, and visit family-run shops and workshops.

Malta's crafts and artisanal traditions are deeply rooted in its cultural fabric. Visit local artisans specializing in lace-making, pottery, and glassblowing, and witness their skills firsthand. Participate in workshops where you can learn these traditional crafts and create your unique souvenirs. The craftspeople's dedication and talent will leave you inspired and connected to Malta's artistic heritage.

9. Museums and Cultural Institutions

Malta is home to a variety of museums and cultural institutions that further enrich your understanding of its history and culture. The National Museum of Archaeology, located in Valletta, houses an exceptional collection of artifacts, including prehistoric tools, ancient pottery, and unique statuettes. The National Museum of Fine Arts showcases artworks spanning various periods, including pieces by prominent Maltese artists.

For a deeper exploration of Malta's maritime history, visit the Malta Maritime Museum in Birgu. Discover the island's seafaring heritage, view antique ship models, and learn about maritime traditions and exploration. Other notable museums include the Malta War Museum, the Malta Postal Museum, and the Museum of Natural History, each offering a unique perspective on different aspects of Malta's cultural heritage.

10. Cultural Experiences Beyond Museums
Immerse yourself in Maltese culture through engaging experiences that go beyond traditional museum visits. Attend a performance by the Malta Philharmonic Orchestra or enjoy a theatrical production at one of Valletta's historic theaters. Experience the vibrant Maltese folk

traditions through live music, traditional dances, and folklore performances. Seek out local festivals and religious processions, such as the Feast of St. Paul's Shipwreck, to witness the islanders' deep-rooted traditions and religious devotion.

11. Literary and Artistic Heritage

Malta's cultural heritage is not limited to its historical and archaeological sites. The island has also nurtured a vibrant literary and artistic scene over the centuries. Explore the works of Maltese writers and poets, such as Dun Karm Psaila, Malta's national poet, or read contemporary works by authors like Immanuel Mifsud and Clare Azzopardi. Visit local art galleries and exhibitions that showcase the diverse talent of Maltese artists, from paintings and sculptures to contemporary installations.

12. Religious Sites and Festivities

Religion plays a significant role in Maltese culture, and the island is dotted with churches, chapels, and religious sites that hold immense historical and spiritual importance. Visit the Basilica of Ta' Pinu in Gozo, a renowned pilgrimage site where locals and visitors seek solace and miracles. Attend religious festivities like Good Friday processions or village feasts, where intricately decorated statues are carried through the streets amidst fervent religious celebrations. These experiences offer a glimpse into Malta's deep-rooted faith and devotion.

13. Maltese Language and Folklore
Maltese, a unique Semitic language with influences from Italian, Arabic, and English, is the national language of Malta. Explore the richness of the Maltese language through local expressions, proverbs, and traditional folk songs. Discover the folklore and mythical tales that have been passed down through generations, such as the legends of the Maltese "Bewsa" (mermaid) or the "Ghar Dalam" (Cave of Darkness).

Engaging with the Maltese language and folklore adds a deeper layer of understanding and appreciation for the local culture.

## 14. Recommended Itineraries and Routes

To make the most of your cultural exploration in Malta, we provide suggested itineraries and routes that ensure you cover the key historical and cultural attractions. Whether you have a few days or a longer stay, these itineraries help you navigate the island efficiently, making sure you don't miss any significant sites. The accompanying maps outline the suggested routes, highlight attractions, and provide essential information to enhance your travel experience.

- Valletta and Three Cities: Immerse yourself in the history and architecture of Valletta and the neighboring Three Cities, including Birgu, Senglea, and Cospicua.

- Temples and Prehistoric Sites: Discover Malta's ancient temples, including Hagar Qim, Mnajdra, Tarxien Temples, and Ggantija Temples, along with other prehistoric sites.
- Cultural Gems of Gozo: Explore the cultural highlights of Gozo, such as Victoria's Citadel, Ta' Pinu Basilica, and the traditional village of Gharb.
- Mdina and Rabat: Uncover the historical treasures of Mdina, Rabat, and nearby attractions like St. Paul's Catacombs and Domus Romana.
- Art and Literature Tour: Immerse yourself in Malta's artistic heritage with visits to art galleries, literary landmarks, and cultural institutions.

15. Cultural Etiquette and Customs

To fully immerse yourself in Malta's culture, it's essential to be mindful of the local customs and etiquette. Maltese people are known for their warm hospitality and respect for traditions. Take the time to greet locals with a friendly "bonġu" (good morning) or "bonus" (good evening) and be open to engaging in conversations and learning about their way of life. When visiting religious sites, dress modestly and be respectful of ongoing ceremonies or prayers. It's customary to remove your shoes before entering someone's home, and it's polite to accept a cup of tea or coffee if offered as a gesture of hospitality.

16. Culinary Traditions and Food Experiences

Malta's culinary scene is a reflection of its rich history and cultural influences. Sample traditional dishes that have stood the test of time, such as rabbit stew (fenkata), ravioli (beef olives), and pastizzi (flaky pastries filled with ricotta or mushy peas). Explore the local food markets, such as Marsaxlokk's Sunday fish market, where you can savor fresh seafood and immerse yourself in the vibrant atmosphere. Consider joining a cooking class to learn how to prepare authentic Maltese dishes using traditional recipes and locally sourced ingredients. Embrace the opportunity to enjoy a traditional Maltese feast (festa) during village festivities, where you can taste a variety of local specialties and experience the lively atmosphere of community celebrations.

## 17. Sustainable and Responsible Tourism

As you explore Malta's history and culture, it's important to be mindful of sustainable and responsible tourism practices. Malta is a small island with a delicate ecosystem, and it's crucial to respect the natural environment and cultural heritage. Opt for eco-friendly activities, such as snorkeling or diving with certified operators who prioritize marine conservation. Support local artisans and businesses that promote sustainable practices and ethically sourced products. Be conscious of your waste and strive to minimize single-use plastics. Consider using public transportation or renting bicycles to reduce your carbon footprint. By adopting responsible tourism practices, you contribute to the preservation of Malta's cultural and natural treasures for future generations.

18. Cultural Events Calendar

To make the most of your visit, familiarize yourself with Malta's cultural events calendar. Throughout the year, the island hosts a wide range of festivals, concerts, art exhibitions, and theatrical performances. Check the schedule for events like the Malta International Arts Festival, Valletta Baroque Festival, Jazz Festival, and Notte Bianca (White Night), a night-long celebration of art and culture. Attending these events provides a unique opportunity to witness the dynamism of Malta's cultural scene and engage with artists from various disciplines.

19. Beyond Malta: Exploring the Sister Islands

While Malta offers a wealth of cultural experiences, don't overlook the sister islands of Gozo and Comino. Gozo, known for its serene ambiance, picturesque landscapes, and historic sites, provides an opportunity to immerse yourself in traditional village life and enjoy the breathtaking coastal scenery. Comino, with its crystal-clear waters and the iconic Blue Lagoon, offers a tranquil escape and an ideal setting for relaxation and water activities. Consider dedicating a portion of your trip to exploring these sister islands and discovering their unique cultural treasures.

20. Resources and Further Reading

To deepen your knowledge of Malta's history and culture, there are various resources and reading materials available. Local history books, travel guides, and archaeological publications provide detailed insights into the island's past. Consider visiting the National Library of Malta in Valletta, which houses an extensive collection of books, manuscripts, and historical documents. Engage with local historians, archaeologists, or cultural experts who can provide unique perspectives and recommendations for further exploration.

21. Personal Reflection and Cultural Exchange

As you explore Malta's history and culture, take the time for personal reflection and cultural exchange. Engage in conversations with locals, listen to their stories, and learn from their experiences. Share your insights and experiences, fostering a mutual exchange of knowledge and understanding. Embrace the opportunity to challenge preconceived notions and broaden your worldview through meaningful interactions with the Maltese people.

## 22. Capturing Memories: Photography and Journaling

To preserve the memories of your cultural exploration in Malta, consider documenting your experiences through photography and journaling. Capture the architectural marvels, vibrant festivals, and everyday moments that resonate with you. Write down your thoughts, reflections, and observations, allowing yourself to relive the cultural encounters long after your trip. These visual and written records serve as a testament to the richness and beauty of Malta's history and culture.

## 23. Lasting Impression: Sharing Your Experience

Upon returning from your journey, share your experience of Malta's history and culture with others. Whether through social media, blog posts, or personal conversations, inspire fellow travelers to explore this captivating destination. Share your insights, recommendations, and favorite cultural highlights, encouraging others to embark on their formative journey through Malta's cultural heritage.

## 24. The Evolving Cultural Landscape

Malta's history and culture continue to evolve and adapt to the changing times. While the island proudly preserves its ancient traditions and landmarks, it also embraces contemporary cultural expressions. Explore the burgeoning art scene, with modern galleries and street art adorning urban spaces. Attend music festivals that showcase local and international artists across a range of genres. Engage with the vibrant theater and performing arts community, attending captivating productions and experimental performances. Witness the fusion of traditional and modern influences that shape Malta's cultural landscape in the present day.

25. Cultural Exchange and Collaboration

Malta's rich history and cultural diversity make it a hub for cultural exchange and collaboration. Artists, writers, musicians, and scholars from around the world come to Malta to draw inspiration, participate in residencies, and collaborate with local creatives. Consider exploring opportunities for cultural exchange, such as attending workshops, participating in artistic collaborations, or joining community initiatives. Engaging with both the local and international artistic community can provide a unique perspective on Malta's culture and foster connections that transcend borders.

26. Digital Engagement and Virtual Experiences

In the digital age, it's easier than ever to engage with Malta's history and culture even before setting foot on the island. Explore online resources, virtual tours, and digital exhibits that bring Malta's cultural heritage to life. Engage with local cultural organizations and institutions through social media platforms, where you can stay updated on events, exhibitions, and cultural initiatives. Participate in online forums or discussions to connect with fellow travelers and cultural enthusiasts who share a passion for Malta's rich heritage.

27. Cultural Sustainability and Preservation Efforts

Preserving Malta's history and culture is a collective responsibility. Learn about the ongoing efforts by local communities, cultural organizations, and heritage institutions to safeguard Malta's cultural treasures. Support initiatives that promote cultural sustainability, such as restoration projects, conservation efforts, and educational programs. By supporting local artisans, craftsmen, and cultural practitioners, you contribute to the preservation and transmission of Malta's traditional skills and knowledge to future generations.

28. Returning to Malta: Rediscovering the Familiar

If you've previously visited Malta, consider returning to deepen your connection with the island's history and culture. Delve into lesser-known attractions, explore new exhibitions or performances, and revisit familiar places with a fresh perspective. Seek out off-the-beaten-path destinations, engage with local communities, and immerse yourself in cultural experiences you may have missed during your previous visit. Rediscover Malta's charm and uncover hidden gems that further enrich your understanding of its captivating heritage.

Malta's history and culture offer a tapestry of experiences that continue to evolve and inspire. By embracing the island's ancient traditions, engaging with contemporary expressions, and supporting cultural sustainability, you become part of the narrative that preserves Malta's rich heritage. Whether through physical exploration, virtual engagement, or returning visits, allow the beauty and depth of Malta's history and culture to captivate your senses and leave an indelible impression on your journey of cultural discovery.

# Chapter 8

## Exciting Water Sports Activities in Malta

Malta's crystal-clear waters and diverse marine life make it a paradise for water sports enthusiasts. In this chapter, we will delve into the thrilling world of water sports in Malta, including scuba diving, snorkeling, and sailing. Whether you're a seasoned diver or a beginner looking to explore the underwater world, Malta offers a range of exhilarating activities to suit every skill level.

1. Scuba Diving:
Malta is renowned for its exceptional scuba diving sites, boasting stunning underwater landscapes, vibrant coral reefs, and intriguing shipwrecks. Here are some key points to consider:

1.1 Diving Centers and Certification:
Numerous professional diving centers cater to divers of all levels. They offer certification courses, guided dives, and equipment rental. Ensure you choose a reputable diving center with experienced instructors.

1.2 Dive Sites:
Malta's dive sites cater to various interests, from underwater caves and tunnels to stunning reefs and historic wrecks. Some popular dive sites include:

- Blue Grotto: Known for its dramatic cliffs and stunning underwater caves, the Blue Grotto offers an awe-inspiring diving experience.
- Ċirkewwa: This site is home to the renowned wreck of the MV Rozi, as well as a range of marine life and underwater rock formations.
- Santa Maria Caves: Located off Comino Island, these caves provide an otherworldly

diving experience, with colorful corals and abundant marine species.

1.3 Wreck Diving:
Malta is a treasure trove for wreck diving enthusiasts. Notable wreck sites include:
- HMS Maori: This World War II destroyer rests just off Valletta's Grand Harbor and offers a captivating glimpse into Malta's history.
- Um El Faroud: Located in the south of Malta, this oil tanker wreck is teeming with marine life and provides a challenging dive experience.

1.4 Marine Life:
Malta's waters are teeming with marine biodiversity, including octopuses, moray eels, groupers, and colorful reef fish. Diving in Malta offers a chance to encounter these fascinating creatures up close.

## 2. Snorkeling:

For those who prefer to stay closer to the water's surface, snorkeling in Malta is a fantastic option. Here's what you need to know:

### 2.1 Snorkeling Locations:

Malta offers an abundance of snorkeling spots with clear waters and vibrant marine life. Some top snorkeling locations include:

- Blue Lagoon (Comino): This iconic spot is a snorkeler's paradise, with its turquoise waters and visibility allowing for breathtaking views of the underwater world.
- St. Peter's Pool (Marsaxlokk): This natural swimming pool offers excellent snorkeling opportunities, with its crystal-clear waters and rocky formations.

### 2.2 Snorkeling Tips:

To make the most of your snorkeling experience in Malta, keep the following tips in mind:

- Use proper snorkeling equipment, including a mask, snorkel, and fins.
- Apply reef-friendly sunscreen to protect your skin and the delicate marine ecosystem.
- Practice responsible snorkeling by avoiding touching or damaging the coral reefs and marine life.

3. Sailing:

Sailing enthusiasts will find Malta's warm Mediterranean waters and gentle sea breezes perfect for exploring the coast and nearby islands. Consider the following aspects:

3.1 Chartering a Boat:

Several companies offer boat charters, ranging from luxury yachts to smaller sailboats. Whether you're an experienced sailor or a beginner, there are options to suit your preferences.

3.2 Sailing Routes:
Malta offers a variety of sailing routes, each with its unique charm. Consider the following popular options:

- Grand Harbor and Marsamxett Harbor: Sail along Valletta's stunning coastline, taking in the impressive fortifications and iconic landmarks.
- Gozo and Comino Islands: Explore the sister islands, discovering secluded coves, hidden beaches, and picturesque anchorages.

3.3 Sailing Events:
If you're interested in sailing events, consider timing your visit to coincide with one of Malta's regattas or boat races. These events showcase the island's seafaring heritage and offer a vibrant atmosphere.

4. Safety Considerations:

4.1 Scuba Diving Safety:
- Always dive with a buddy and ensure you have the necessary certifications and training for the dive site's difficulty level.
- Follow the instructions of your dive instructor or guide and pay attention to dive briefings and safety protocols.
- Check your equipment before each dive and maintain proper buoyancy control to protect yourself and the marine environment.
- Stay within your comfort zone and avoid pushing your limits to prevent accidents or injuries.

4.2 Snorkeling Safety:
- Choose snorkeling spots suitable for your skill level and pay attention to local weather and sea conditions.
- Familiarize yourself with potential hazards, such as strong currents or boat

traffic, and avoid snorkeling in restricted areas.
- Use a snorkel vest or flotation device if needed, especially if you're less confident in the water.
- Keep a safe distance from coral reefs to prevent accidental damage and avoid touching marine life.

4.3 Sailing Safety:
- Before embarking on a sailing trip, ensure you have a good understanding of the boat's operation and safety equipment.
- Check weather conditions and tides before setting sail and be prepared for potential changes in the weather.
- Maintain situational awareness while sailing, especially in busy areas or near underwater hazards.
- Follow navigation rules and regulations, including right of way and speed limits, to ensure safe and responsible sailing.

5. Rental and Tour Operators:

5.1 Scuba Diving:
- Research and choose reputable diving centers that have experienced instructors and well-maintained equipment.
- Read reviews and seek recommendations from fellow divers to ensure a safe and enjoyable diving experience.
- Inquire about the range of dive sites they offer, equipment rental options, and any additional services or certifications available.

5.2 Snorkeling:
- If you're not comfortable snorkeling on your own, consider joining a guided snorkeling tour that provides equipment and guidance.
- Research snorkeling tour operators that have knowledgeable guides and prioritize safety.
- Ensure the tour operator follows responsible snorkeling practices, such as

providing instructions on marine conservation and avoiding damage to coral reefs.

5.3 Sailing:
- When chartering a boat, choose reputable companies that have well-maintained vessels and experienced skippers.
- Inquire about safety equipment onboard, including life jackets and navigation aids.
- Ensure the charter company provides necessary safety instructions and guidelines for operating the boat.

6. Recommended Itineraries:

6.1 Scuba Diving:
- For avid divers, consider a week-long itinerary that includes dives in diverse locations such as the Blue Grotto, Ċirkewwa, and the wrecks of HMS Maori and Um El Faroud.

- Allocate time for rest days to prevent fatigue and allow for decompression after deep dives.

6.2 Snorkeling:
- Plan a day trip to Comino's Blue Lagoon for snorkeling in its crystal-clear waters and exploring the underwater caves.
- Combine snorkeling with a visit to St. Peter's Pool in Marsaxlokk to enjoy a relaxing day by the sea.

6.3 Sailing:
- Embark on a sailing adventure around Malta and Gozo, spending a few days exploring the coastlines, visiting secluded bays, and docking at picturesque harbors.
- Consider including stops at the island of Comino and its Blue Lagoon for a refreshing swim and snorkeling session.

Water sports enthusiasts visiting Malta can indulge in the thrill of scuba diving, snorkeling, and sailing in the stunning Mediterranean waters. With proper planning, adherence to safety guidelines, and choosing reputable operators, you can make the most of these exhilarating activities while enjoying the natural beauty and rich marine life that Malta has to offer. Whether you choose to dive into the depths, snorkel near vibrant reefs, or sail along the captivating coastline, the water sports experiences in Malta are sure to create lasting memories.

# Suggestions for Hiking and Cycling Routes, with Descriptions of Scenic Trails

Malta's diverse landscapes, rugged coastline, and rolling countryside make it an ideal destination for outdoor enthusiasts. In this chapter, we will explore the best hiking and cycling routes that showcase the natural beauty and cultural heritage of the Maltese islands. Whether you prefer a stroll or an adrenaline-fueled adventure, there is something for everyone to enjoy.

1. Majjistral Nature and History Park:
Located on the northwest coast of Malta, Majjistral Nature and History Park offers a range of hiking trails that lead you through dramatic cliffs, hidden coves, and lush valleys. One popular route is the Fomm ir-Rih Trail, which starts in the village of Baħrija and takes you down to the secluded Fomm ir-Rih Bay. The trail offers breathtaking views of the Mediterranean

Sea and the opportunity to explore ancient Roman baths along the way.

2. Dingli Cliffs:
For a captivating coastal hike, head to the Dingli Cliffs, situated on the southwestern coast of Malta. These dramatic cliffs offer stunning panoramic views of the Mediterranean Sea and the surrounding countryside. The Dingli Cliffs Circular Walk is a popular choice, taking you on a circular route from Dingli village, passing through terraced fields, chapels, and ancient cart ruts. Make sure to visit the Dingli Radar Station for a unique perspective on the cliffs.

3. Victoria Lines:
For history enthusiasts and nature lovers, the Victoria Lines trail is a must. These defensive fortifications, stretching across the island of Malta, offer a challenging and rewarding hiking experience. The trail covers approximately 12 kilometers from Madliena to Fomm ir-Riħ, passing through

various terrains and landscapes. Along the way, you'll encounter breathtaking views, fortifications, and historical sites that provide insight into Malta's military history.

4. Gozo Coastal Walk:
If you're visiting Gozo, the smaller sister island of Malta, don't miss the Gozo Coastal Walk. This scenic trail offers a glimpse of Gozo's stunning cliffs, secluded bays, and charming villages. Starting from the picturesque village of Marsalforn, you can follow the trail to Xwejni Bay, passing by the iconic salt pans and the ruggedly beautiful Ramla Bay. The walk continues along the coast, leading you to the historic citadel in Victoria (also known as Rabat).

5. Delimara Peninsula:
For a lesser-known hiking gem, head to the Delimara Peninsula in the southeast of Malta. This area is a nature lover's paradise, boasting rugged coastal paths, hidden caves, and breathtaking views. The Delimara

Peninsula Circular Trail begins in Marsaxlokk and takes you along the coastline, passing through Delimara Point and St. Peter's Pool, a natural swimming spot renowned for its crystal-clear waters. The trail offers a mix of coastal scenery and rural landscapes.

6. Cycling in the Maltese Countryside:
If cycling is more your style, Malta offers a variety of routes that allow you to explore the scenic countryside at your own pace. The Zebbug to Mgarr Route is a popular choice, taking you through charming rural villages and picturesque vineyards. The route offers a mix of flat terrain and gentle hills, making it suitable for cyclists of all skill levels. Along the way, you can stop at local farms and wineries to sample delicious Maltese produce.

7. Coastal Cycling in Gozo:
Gozo's compact size and stunning coastal scenery make it a cyclist's paradise. One

recommended route is the Xlendi to Marsalforn Coastal Ride, which takes you along the scenic coast, passing through quaint villages, rugged cliffs, and sandy beaches. This route offers a mix of flat and hilly terrain, with plenty of opportunities to stop and enjoy the picturesque views or take a dip in the turquoise waters.

8. Comino Island Hike and Bike:
Comino, the smallest of the three main islands in Malta, offers a unique setting for hiking and cycling enthusiasts. The island's compact size makes it ideal for exploration on foot or by bike. Start your adventure by taking a ferry to Comino and renting a bicycle from one of the local providers. Begin your journey by following the scenic coastal road, passing by the famous Blue Lagoon with its crystal-clear waters. As you venture further inland, you'll discover rugged trails that lead you through pristine landscapes and secluded beaches. Don't miss the opportunity to hike up to the Santa

Marija Tower, an ancient watchtower that offers panoramic views of the island. With its tranquil ambiance and untouched beauty, Comino is a hidden gem for outdoor enthusiasts.

9. Mellieha to Golden Bay Coastal Trail:
Mellieha, a charming town in the northern part of Malta, serves as the starting point for a picturesque coastal trail to Golden Bay. This trail offers breathtaking views of the Mediterranean Sea and takes you through diverse landscapes, including rocky cliffs, sandy beaches, and rolling hills. Begin your journey from Mellieha Bay and follow the marked path that hugs the coastline. Along the way, you'll encounter hidden coves, interesting rock formations, and the historic Red Tower, a 17th-century fortification. Arriving at Golden Bay, you can relax on the sandy beach or reward yourself with a refreshing swim in the turquoise waters.

10. Hiking in Gozo's Inland Gems:

Gozo's inland areas are a treasure trove of natural beauty and cultural heritage, offering fantastic hiking opportunities away from the coast. One recommended trail is the Nadur to Xaghra Circular Walk, which takes you through scenic valleys, lush farmland, and historic sites. Begin your hike in the village of Nadur and follow the trail through fertile fields and vineyards. Along the way, you'll pass by the fascinating Xaghra Stone Circle, an ancient archaeological site, and the imposing Ggantija Temples, a UNESCO World Heritage site. The trail also offers panoramic views of the picturesque Ramla Bay, known for its red-golden sand.

11. Gozo Coastal Cycling Odyssey:
For avid cyclists looking for a more challenging adventure, the Gozo Coastal Cycling Odyssey is an exhilarating route that circumnavigates the entire island. Start from Mgarr Harbour and embark on a journey along the rugged coastline, passing

through charming fishing villages, dramatic cliffs, and panoramic viewpoints. This route offers a mix of steep climbs and exhilarating descents, providing a thrilling and rewarding experience for experienced cyclists. Along the way, take breaks to explore hidden beaches, visit historical sites, and savor the delicious local cuisine in the quaint village eateries.

Maps, Itineraries, and Suggested Routes:
To enhance your hiking and cycling experience in Malta, it's highly recommended to use detailed maps, itineraries, and suggested routes. These resources will help you navigate the trails, plan your journey effectively, and make the most of your time on the islands. You can find reliable maps and guidebooks at local tourist information centers or download digital maps and GPS routes from reputable online sources. Additionally, consider joining organized tours or hiring experienced guides who can provide

valuable insights and ensure your safety throughout your outdoor adventures.

Malta's diverse landscapes and scenic trails offer an abundance of opportunities for hiking and cycling enthusiasts. From coastal walks with panoramic views to inland hikes that showcase Malta's cultural heritage, the islands provide a range of outdoor experiences for all skill levels. By exploring the suggested routes and utilizing maps and itineraries, you can immerse yourself in the natural beauty of Malta, discover hidden gems, and create unforgettable memories on your outdoor escapades. So grab your hiking boots or hop on a bicycle, and let the trails of Malta lead you to remarkable adventures.
When embarking on hiking or cycling adventures in Malta, it's important to come prepared. Wear comfortable footwear, carry sufficient water, and dress appropriately for the weather conditions. Remember to check for any trail closures or restrictions before

setting out and respect the natural environment by leaving no trace.

# Thrilling Experiences in Malta: Cliff Jumping, Rock Climbing, and Horseback Riding

Malta isn't just about beautiful beaches and historical sites; it also offers exhilarating activities for adventure enthusiasts. In this chapter, we will explore thrilling experiences such as cliff jumping, rock climbing, and horseback riding, providing you with detailed information to embark on unforgettable adventures.

1. Cliff Jumping:
Cliff jumping in Malta offers an adrenaline rush combined with breathtaking coastal scenery. Here's what you need to know:

- Popular Locations: The Blue Grotto, located on the southern coast of Malta, is a renowned spot for cliff jumping. It features towering cliffs and deep blue waters, making it an ideal destination for thrill-seekers.

- Safety Considerations: Cliff jumping can be dangerous, so it's crucial to prioritize safety. Consider the following precautions:
  - Assess the height and depth of the jump before leaping.
  - Always jump feet-first to minimize the risk of injuries.
  - Check the water for any potential hazards, such as rocks or debris.
  - Only attempt cliff jumping if you have previous experience or under the guidance of a professional.

- Local Guidance: Consider joining a guided tour or seeking advice from locals who are familiar with the area. They can provide valuable insights into the best locations, safety measures, and potential challenges.

2. Rock Climbing:
Malta offers a diverse range of rock climbing opportunities, catering to both beginners and experienced climbers. Here's what you should know:

- Climbing Areas: Malta's limestone cliffs provide excellent rock climbing opportunities. Some popular climbing areas include Dingli Cliffs, Wied Babu, and Ghar Lapsi. Each location offers unique rock formations and varying levels of difficulty.

- Equipment: Bring your climbing gear or consider renting from local outfitters. Essential equipment includes harnesses, helmets, climbing shoes, and ropes. Ensure your equipment is in good condition and properly maintained.

- Safety and Access: Check the access regulations for each climbing area, as some may require permits or have restrictions due to nesting birds or conservation efforts. Prioritize safety by climbing with a partner, using proper techniques, and staying within your skill level.

- Guided Experiences: If you're new to rock climbing or want to explore the best routes, consider hiring a local guide or joining a climbing tour. They can provide instruction, equipment, and insider knowledge of the best climbing spots in Malta.

3. Horseback Riding:
Exploring Malta's beautiful landscapes on horseback offers a unique and memorable experience. Here's what you need to know about horseback riding in Malta:

- Equestrian Centers: Malta has several equestrian centers that offer horseback riding experiences for all levels of riders. These centers provide well-trained horses, safety equipment, and knowledgeable guides.

- Scenic Routes: Enjoy leisurely rides through scenic countryside, along coastal paths, or even on the beach. Popular destinations for horseback riding include Bidnija, Pembroke, and Golden Bay.

- Riding Lessons: If you're a beginner or want to improve your riding skills, many equestrian centers offer lessons and training sessions with experienced instructors. Take the opportunity to learn about horsemanship and bond with these magnificent animals.

- Sunset Rides: For a romantic and picturesque experience, consider booking a sunset ride, where you can enjoy breathtaking views as the sun dips below the horizon.

- Health and Safety: Prioritize your safety by wearing appropriate riding gear, including helmets. Follow the instructions of your guide and be mindful of your horse's needs and behavior during the ride.

Remember to book horseback riding experiences in advance, especially during peak tourist seasons, to secure your spot.
- Environmental Responsibility: When engaging in these thrilling activities, it's important to respect the environment and wildlife. Avoid disturbing natural habitats, refrain from littering, and follow any guidelines or restrictions in place to preserve the beauty of the Maltese landscape.

- Weather Considerations: Keep an eye on the weather conditions before participating in any of these activities. Unfavorable weather, such as strong winds or rough sea conditions, can make cliff jumping or horseback riding unsafe. Always prioritize your safety and follow any recommendations or warnings from local authorities or activity providers.

- Local Operators and Guides: To ensure a safe and enjoyable experience, consider engaging the services of experienced local operators or guides. They can provide expert guidance, and valuable insights, and ensure that you have access to the necessary equipment and knowledge to make the most of your adventure.

- Duration and Fitness Level: Take into account the duration and physical demands of each activity when planning your itinerary. Cliff jumping and rock climbing may require a certain level of fitness and strength, while horseback riding can vary in intensity depending on the chosen route and pace. Be realistic about your abilities and choose activities that align with your fitness level and comfort zone.

- Photography and Souvenirs: Don't forget to capture your thrilling moments through photographs or videos to preserve the memories of your adventure. Many activity providers offer photo or video packages for purchase, allowing you to relive those adrenaline-pumping experiences long after you've left Malta.

- Local Tips and Insider Knowledge: When engaging in thrilling activities, it's always helpful to gather local tips and insider knowledge. Talk to locals, guides, or fellow adventure enthusiasts to gain insights into the best spots, lesser-known routes, and any additional precautions or recommendations. They can provide valuable information that enhances your experience and ensures you make the most of your time in Malta.

- Combination of Activities: Consider combining multiple thrilling activities to create a dynamic and diverse adventure itinerary. For example, start your day with a rock climbing session, followed by a refreshing cliff jump into the crystal-clear waters, and conclude with a leisurely horseback ride along the coastline. By combining activities, you can enjoy a well-rounded and exhilarating experience.

- Group or Solo Adventures: Decide whether you prefer to embark on these thrilling experiences as part of a group or on your own. Joining a group tour or activity can provide a sense of camaraderie and the opportunity to meet like-minded individuals. On the other hand, solo adventures allow for more flexibility and the freedom to tailor the experience to your preferences. Choose the option that aligns with your comfort level and desired level of independence.

- Booking in Advance: To secure your spot and ensure availability, especially during peak seasons, it's advisable to book these activities in advance. Cliff jumping tours, rock climbing sessions, and horseback riding experiences may have limited spaces, so plan accordingly and make reservations ahead of time to avoid disappointment.

- Personal Limits and Comfort Zones: While seeking thrilling experiences, it's important to be aware of your personal limits and comfort zones. Everyone has different levels of risk tolerance and physical abilities. Listen to your intuition and assess the risks involved in each activity. If you feel uncomfortable or unsure about any aspect, it's okay to opt for alternative options or modify the activity to suit your preferences.

- Building Skills and Progression: If you're new to these activities, consider starting with beginner-friendly options and gradually building your skills and confidence. Take rock climbing lessons, practice cliff jumping from lower heights before attempting higher jumps, and choose horseback riding routes suitable for your experience level. By progressing at a comfortable pace, you can safely enjoy these activities while developing new skills along the way.

- Capturing the Moment: Document your thrilling adventures by capturing photographs or videos to preserve the excitement and beauty of the experiences. Bring along a waterproof camera or a reliable camera mount for action shots while cliff jumping or rock climbing. However, always prioritize safety and ensure your equipment is secure during the activities.

- Post-Adventure Relaxation: After indulging in thrilling activities, take some time to relax and rejuvenate. Malta offers numerous opportunities for relaxation, such as visiting a spa, lounging on a tranquil beach, or enjoying a leisurely meal at a seaside restaurant. Treat yourself to some well-deserved downtime to recharge before your next adventure.

- Responsible Adventure Tourism: As you embark on thrilling experiences, it's essential to practice responsible adventure tourism. Respect the environment, wildlife, and local communities by adhering to regulations, avoiding damage to natural habitats, and supporting sustainable tourism initiatives. Leave no trace behind and ensure that future visitors can also enjoy the beauty of Malta's natural wonders.

- Weather and Seasonal Considerations: Pay attention to the weather conditions and seasonal variations when planning your thrilling adventures. Some activities may be weather-dependent, with certain seasons providing more favorable conditions. For example, cliff jumping and horseback riding are generally more enjoyable during the warm summer months, while rock climbing may be better suited for spring or autumn when temperatures are milder. Stay informed about any seasonal restrictions, closures, or weather-related factors that may impact your chosen activities.

- Fitness and Preparation: Engaging in thrilling activities requires a certain level of physical fitness and preparation. Before your trip, consider incorporating exercises and activities that improve your strength, endurance, and flexibility. Focus on cardiovascular fitness, core strength, and upper body strength, as these will be particularly beneficial for activities like cliff jumping and rock climbing. Engaging in regular physical activity and maintaining a healthy lifestyle will enhance your overall experience and reduce the risk of injuries.

- Embracing the Unexpected: While planning and preparation are crucial, don't be afraid to embrace the unexpected. Sometimes, the most thrilling experiences come from spontaneous moments or unplanned detours. Allow room for flexibility in your itinerary, be open to new opportunities, and seize the chance to try something new that may not have been on your original agenda. Embracing the unexpected can lead to incredible adventures and unforgettable memories.

By delving into the details, expanding on important considerations, and providing practical advice, you can fully immerse yourself in the thrilling experiences Malta has to offer. Whether you're cliff jumping into crystal-clear waters, scaling limestone cliffs, or galloping along scenic landscapes on horseback, these exhilarating activities will leave you with a profound sense of adventure and a deeper connection to the captivating beauty of Malta.

By embracing the thrilling experiences that Malta offers, you'll have the opportunity to engage with the islands uniquely and unforgettably. Whether you're leaping a cliff, scaling magnificent limestone formations, or exploring the landscapes on horseback, these adventures will add an extra layer of excitement and discovery to your Maltese journey. Embrace the challenges, soak in the awe-inspiring scenery, and create memories that will last a lifetime.

Note: Always prioritize your safety and follow the guidance of trained professionals when participating in these activities. Conditions and regulations may change, so ensure you stay updated with the latest information and guidelines.

Malta's thrilling experiences like cliff jumping, rock climbing, and horseback riding offer adventure seekers an opportunity to explore the islands uniquely and excitingly. Whether you're plunging into crystal-clear waters, conquering limestone cliffs, or riding through picturesque landscapes, these activities will undoubtedly leave you with lasting memories and a sense of exhilaration. Take the necessary safety precautions, seek local guidance when needed, and embrace the adventure that awaits you in Malta.

# Exploring the Outdoors: Diving, Hiking, and Adventure in Malta

Malta offers a wealth of opportunities for outdoor enthusiasts to indulge in thrilling adventures and immerse themselves in the stunning natural beauty of the islands. This chapter will guide you through the best diving sites, hiking trails, and outdoor adventure spots, providing detailed information and suggestions to help you make the most of your outdoor exploration in Malta.

1. Diving in Malta:
Malta is renowned for its crystal-clear waters and abundant marine life, making it a paradise for divers. The island boasts numerous diving sites, each with its unique charm and underwater wonders. Here are some of the top diving spots in Malta:

- Blue Grotto: Located on the southern coast of Malta, the Blue Grotto offers an enchanting diving experience. Dive into the deep blue waters, explore intricate caves, and marvel at the vibrant marine life.

- Cirkewwa: Situated in the northwestern part of Malta, Cirkewwa is a popular diving site known for its breathtaking underwater landscape and the famous wreck of the MV Rozi.

- Gozo and Comino: The sister islands of Gozo and Comino also offer fantastic diving opportunities. Explore the underwater caves of Gozo, such as the stunning Blue Hole, or discover the rich marine biodiversity around Comino's coast.

Each diving site has different depths and difficulty levels, catering to divers of all skill levels. It is advisable to go diving with a certified diving center or instructor who can guide you through the sites and ensure your safety.

2. Hiking Trails in Malta:
Malta's diverse landscapes provide excellent opportunities for hiking enthusiasts to explore scenic trails, rugged cliffs, and picturesque countryside. Lace up your hiking boots and embark on these captivating trails in Malta:

- Dingli Cliffs: Enjoy a breathtaking coastal hike along the Dingli Cliffs, located on the western coast of Malta. Marvel at the panoramic views of the Mediterranean Sea and the rugged limestone cliffs that drop dramatically into the azure waters below.
- Victoria Lines: Follow the historic Victoria Lines, a defensive fortification that stretches across the island of Malta. This scenic trail takes you through valleys, and countryside, and offers stunning views of the surrounding landscape.
- Fomm ir-Riħ: This challenging hike on the western coast of Malta rewards hikers with magnificent vistas of cliffs, secluded bays, and the untouched beauty of nature. Be

prepared for steep descents and rugged terrain.

Gozo, the sister island of Malta, also boasts incredible hiking trails:

- Azure Window to Ramla Bay: Embark on a memorable coastal hike from the iconic Azure Window (formerly) to the golden sands of Ramla Bay. Traverse through scenic landscapes and enjoy breathtaking views of the Mediterranean Sea.
- Ta' Ċenċ Cliffs: Explore the wild beauty of Gozo on the Ta' Ċenċ Cliffs trail. This challenging hike takes you along the dramatic cliffs, offering uninterrupted views of the surrounding sea and countryside.
- Xlendi to Marsalforn: Experience the coastal charm of Gozo with this scenic trail that connects the picturesque towns of Xlendi and Marsalforn. Enjoy stunning views of the cliffs, rocky beaches, and shimmering Mediterranean waters.

3. Outdoor Adventure Spots:
In addition to diving and hiking, Malta offers various thrilling outdoor activities for adventure enthusiasts:

- Rock Climbing: Scale the vertical cliffs of Malta and Gozo, which provide excellent rock climbing opportunities for both beginners and experienced climbers. Various climbing routes are available, offering different levels of difficulty.
- Cliff Jumping: If you seek an adrenaline rush, try cliff jumping at spots like Għar Lapsi or St. Peter's Pool. Plunge into the crystal-clear waters from natural platforms, surrounded by breathtaking coastal scenery.
- Kayaking and Stand-Up Paddleboarding: Explore Malta's coastline and hidden coves by kayaking or stand-up paddleboarding. Rent equipment and embark on a self-guided adventure or join a guided tour to discover secluded spots and marine life.

4. Recommended Itineraries:

To help you plan your outdoor adventures, here are two suggested itineraries that cover a range of activities and highlight the best of Malta's natural beauty:

- Adventure Extravaganza (7 days):
  - Days 1-3: Dive into the underwater world with dives at Blue Grotto, Cirkewwa, and Gozo's top dive sites.
  - Days 4-5: Embark on thrilling hikes along Dingli Cliffs, Victoria Lines, and explore the hidden trails of Gozo.
  - Days 6-7: Engage in outdoor activities such as rock climbing, cliff jumping, or kayaking.

- Nature Escape (5 days):
  - Days 1-2: Discover Malta's marine treasures with dives at Blue Grotto, Cirkewwa, and Comino's diving sites.
  - Days 3-4: Immerse yourself in nature with hikes along Dingli Cliffs, Fomm ir-Riħ, and explore Gozo's scenic trails.

- Day 5: Indulge in an outdoor adventure of your choice, such as rock climbing, cliff jumping, or kayaking.

Remember to check the weather conditions, local regulations, and consult with experienced guides or tour operators for the best outdoor adventure experience. Stay safe and enjoy the remarkable natural landscapes that Malta has to offer.

5. Maps for Outdoor Adventures:
To assist you in navigating the outdoor adventure spots in Malta, here are detailed maps highlighting the diving sites, hiking trails, and key outdoor attractions:

- Diving Sites Map: This map features the top diving sites in Malta, including the Blue Grotto, Cirkewwa, Gozo, and Comino. It provides locations, depths, and highlights of each site, allowing you to plan your diving adventures accordingly.

- Hiking Trails Map: Discover the beauty of Malta's hiking trails with this comprehensive map. It outlines the routes for Dingli Cliffs, Victoria Lines, Fomm ir-Riħ, and the captivating trails in Gozo. The map includes trailheads, distances, and points of interest along the way.

- Outdoor Adventure Map: This map showcases the exciting outdoor adventure spots across Malta. It marks rock climbing areas, cliff jumping locations, and recommended spots for kayaking and stand-up paddleboarding. Use this map to plan your thrilling escapades.]

These maps will serve as valuable resources, ensuring that you can navigate the outdoor adventure sites with ease and make the most of your time in Malta.

6. Additional Tips for Outdoor Adventures:

To enhance your outdoor experiences in Malta, consider the following tips:

- Safety First: Prioritize your safety by wearing the appropriate gear, following diving or climbing guidelines, and being cautious when exploring rugged terrains or engaging in adventurous activities.
- Local Guidance: Seek advice from experienced local guides or tour operators who possess extensive knowledge of the outdoor sites. They can offer valuable insights, ensure your safety, and enhance your overall experience.
- Equipment Rental: If you don't have your equipment, numerous shops and rental centers across Malta offer diving gear, hiking equipment, kayaks, and more. Renting equipment is a convenient option for travelers who wish to engage in outdoor activities without carrying bulky gear.
- Respect Nature and Wildlife: As you explore Malta's outdoor spaces, remember to be respectful of the environment, wildlife,

and local communities. Follow the "Leave No Trace" principles, dispose of waste responsibly, and avoid disturbing natural habitats.
- Check Weather Conditions: Before embarking on any outdoor adventure, check the weather forecast to ensure optimal conditions for your chosen activity. Unfavorable weather can impact safety and visibility, so plan accordingly.

By following these tips, you can have an unforgettable outdoor adventure experience in Malta while prioritizing safety, respecting nature, and creating lasting memories.

Malta's outdoor adventure scene offers a plethora of opportunities for divers, hikers, and thrill-seekers. Explore the underwater wonders, traverse scenic trails, and immerse yourself in the natural beauty that Malta has to offer. With detailed maps, suggested itineraries, and essential tips, you're well-equipped to embark on your outdoor adventures and create unforgettable experiences in this captivating Mediterranean destination.

# Chapter 9

## Savory Delights: Maltese Cuisine

Welcome to a culinary adventure through the flavors of Malta. Maltese cuisine is a delightful fusion of Mediterranean influences, blending traditional recipes with hints of Italian, North African, and Middle Eastern gastronomy. In this chapter, we will explore the unique dishes, local specialties, and vibrant food culture that make Maltese cuisine a true culinary delight.

1. Introduction to Maltese Cuisine:
Maltese cuisine reflects the island's history and geography, with a focus on fresh ingredients, hearty flavors, and simple yet delicious recipes. The cuisine celebrates the abundance of seafood, locally grown produce, and the unique cultural heritage of the Maltese people.

2. Must-Try Dishes and Local Specialties:

a. Pastizzi: Start your culinary journey with pastizzi, a popular Maltese street food. These savory pastries are filled with either ricotta cheese (pastizzi tal-ricotta) or a mixture of mashed peas (pastizzi tal-piżelli). Enjoy them hot and flaky, and savor the flavors of the filling.

b. Fenkata (Rabbit Stew): A true national dish, fenkata is a hearty rabbit stew cooked in a rich tomato-based sauce. The tender meat is marinated and slow-cooked with garlic, herbs, and sometimes wine. Fenkata is typically enjoyed as a communal meal, bringing family and friends together.

c. Ftira: A traditional Maltese bread, ftira is a must-try. It is round, crusty, and topped with various ingredients, similar to a pizza. Sample ftira topped with fresh tomatoes, olives, capers, tuna, and local cheese for a flavorsome experience.

d. Aljotta: Seafood lovers will relish aljotta, a flavorful fish soup. Made with a variety of local fish, garlic, tomatoes, onions, herbs, and a touch of lemon, this dish showcases the freshness of Malta's coastal waters.

e. Stuffat tal-Fenek (Rabbit Stew with Red Wine): Similar to fenkata, this rabbit stew is cooked in a rich red wine sauce. The slow cooking process allows the flavors to meld together, resulting in a tender and succulent dish.

f. Timpana: Timpana is a baked pasta dish with a twist. Macaroni is combined with a meaty tomato sauce, eggs, and a layer of pastry on top. The result is a comforting and indulgent delight that will satisfy any pasta lover.

3. Culinary Experiences and Local Markets:
a. Marsaxlokk Fish Market: Visit the vibrant fishing village of Marsaxlokk on a Sunday morning to experience the lively fish

market. Stroll along the waterfront and explore the colorful stalls filled with a variety of fresh fish and seafood.

b. Local Farmhouses: Many Maltese farmhouses offer authentic cooking experiences, where you can learn to prepare traditional dishes under the guidance of local chefs. Engage in hands-on cooking lessons, discover the secrets of Maltese ingredients, and enjoy a delicious meal afterward.

c. Food Festivals: Plan your visit to coincide with one of Malta's food festivals. The Malta International Food Festival and the Żejtun Olive Oil Festival are perfect opportunities to indulge in a wide array of local and international cuisine while experiencing the festive atmosphere.

4. Traditional Sweets and Desserts:
a. Kannoli: Kannoli, or cannoli, are sweet pastry shells filled with a creamy ricotta

cheese mixture. These delightful treats are often enjoyed during special occasions and festivals.

b. Helwa tat-Tork: Helwa tat-Tork, also known as Turkish Delight, is a popular sweet made from sugar, and nuts, and sometimes flavored with rosewater or citrus. These chewy delights are a favorite among locals and visitors alike.

c. Imqaret: Imqaret are sweet pastries made with date-filled pastry dough. Deep-fried to perfection, they are best enjoyed warm with a dusting of powdered sugar.

5. Recommended Restaurants and Culinary Hotspots:
- Palazzo Preca: Located in Valletta, Palazzo Preca offers a refined dining experience with a focus on fresh seafood and innovative Mediterranean dishes.

- Ta' Philip: This family-run restaurant in Marsaxlokk specializes in traditional Maltese cuisine, including fresh fish and hearty stews.

- Rubino: Situated in the heart of Valletta, Rubino is renowned for its rustic Maltese dishes and warm, welcoming atmosphere.

- Ta' Kris: A hidden gem in Sliema, Ta' Kris serves authentic Maltese cuisine with a creative twist, using local ingredients and traditional recipes.

6. Wine and Local Beverages:
Malta has a budding wine industry, producing unique and flavorful wines. Take the opportunity to taste local varieties such as Gellewza and Ghirghentina, and visit vineyards such as Meridiana Wine Estate and Delicata Winery for tours and tastings. Don't forget to sample the local liqueur, the sweet and herbal Bajtra (Prickly Pear

liqueur), as well as the refreshing Kinnie, a bittersweet citrus soda.

Maltese cuisine is a delightful blend of flavors, influenced by centuries of cultural exchange and the abundance of local ingredients. From savory pastries to hearty stews, traditional sweets, and innovative dishes, exploring Malta's culinary landscape is a treat for the senses. Embrace the flavors, savor each bite, and immerse yourself in the rich gastronomic heritage of the Maltese Islands.

7. Food Markets and Local Produce:
Explore the local markets to experience the vibrant array of fresh produce, spices, and local delicacies. The Marsaxlokk Fish Market is a must-visit, where you can witness the lively atmosphere and find an assortment of seafood straight from the fishermen's boats. The Valletta Market, also known as the Is-Suq Tal-Belt, offers a diverse selection of fruits, vegetables,

cheese, spices, and other local products. Engage with the friendly vendors, learn about the ingredients, and bring home some flavors of Malta.

8. Culinary Workshops and Cooking Classes:

Immerse yourself in Maltese cuisine by participating in culinary workshops and cooking classes. Various establishments, such as the Mediterranean Culinary Academy and local farmhouses, offer hands-on experiences where you can learn to prepare traditional dishes from expert chefs. Discover the art of making pastizzi, Venkata, and other Maltese specialties. From selecting fresh ingredients to mastering cooking techniques, these classes provide an interactive and educational way to delve deeper into the local culinary traditions.

9. Traditional Food Festivals:
Malta hosts several food festivals throughout the year, celebrating the richness of its cuisine. The Malta International Food Festival, held in Valletta, showcases a wide range of international and local dishes, allowing visitors to indulge in a gastronomic feast. The Żejtun Olive Oil Festival highlights the significance of olives and olive oil in Maltese cuisine, offering tastings, cooking demonstrations, and cultural performances. These festivals provide a vibrant atmosphere to engage with the local food scene and discover new flavors.

10. Exploring Maltese Wine:
Malta's wine culture is thriving, with vineyards producing unique varietals. Embark on a wine-tasting journey and explore the flavors of Maltese wine. Visit wineries such as Meridiana Wine Estate and Delicata Winery, where you can take guided tours, learn about the winemaking process,

and sample a range of red, white, and rosé wines. The indigenous grape varieties, such as Gellewza and Ghirghentina, offer distinctive flavors that reflect the island's terroir. Appreciate the craftsmanship and passion behind Maltese wine production.

11. Unique Local Beverages:
In addition to wine, Malta offers a range of unique local beverages to tantalize your taste buds. Try the famous Maltese soft drink called Kinnie, made from bitter oranges and aromatic herbs. Its refreshing and distinctive flavor makes it a popular choice among locals and visitors alike. For those seeking a taste of traditional liqueur, indulge in Bajtra, a sweet and aromatic Prickly Pear liqueur. It's fruity notes and smooth texture provide a delightful experience and a perfect way to end a meal.

12. Sustainable and Farm-to-Table Experiences:

Malta's commitment to sustainability and local produce is evident in its farm-to-table experiences. Discover restaurants and cafes that prioritize sourcing ingredients from local farmers and fishermen, ensuring freshness and supporting the local economy. These establishments offer menus that change with the seasons, showcasing the best of what the island has to offer. Enjoy a true farm-to-fork experience, knowing that you are contributing to the preservation of the local food culture and environment.

The culinary landscape of Malta is a treasure trove of flavors, traditions, and unique experiences. From indulging in traditional dishes to exploring local markets, participating in cooking classes, and savoring Maltese wines, your journey through Maltese cuisine promises to be a memorable one. Embrace the warmth of the people, the richness of the flavors, and the vibrant food culture that makes Malta a haven for food enthusiasts. Allow your taste buds to be delighted as you discover the authentic flavors and culinary heritage of this captivating Mediterranean destination.

13. Exploring Maltese Cheese and Dairy Products:

Malta boasts a variety of delicious cheese and dairy products that are worth discovering. Try the Ġbejna, a traditional goat's cheese with a creamy texture and a tangy flavor. It is often enjoyed fresh or aged with herbs and spices. Tal-Maħlut is another popular cheese made from sheep's milk, known for its unique flavor and crumbly texture. Visit local cheese farms and dairies, such as the Ta' Mena Dairy Farm and the Benna Dairy, to witness the cheese-making process and sample different varieties.

14. Seafood Delicacies:

Given its island location, it's no surprise that Malta offers a bounty of seafood delicacies.

Indulge in fresh fish like lampuki (dorado), dentex, and sea bream, prepared in various mouthwatering ways. Taste the traditional lampuki pie, a savory pastry filled with fish, vegetables, and herbs. Another popular dish is aljotta, a flavorful fish soup made with tomatoes, garlic, onions, and a medley of herbs and spices. Explore seafood-focused restaurants, particularly those along the coast, for a truly memorable dining experience.

15. Sweet Temptations:
Maltese desserts are a delightful way to end a meal. Sample the kannoli, crispy pastry tubes filled with a sweet ricotta cheese mixture and often topped with candied fruit. Imqaret, deep-fried date-filled pastries, are a local favorite. Their sticky sweetness and crunchy exterior create a perfect balance of flavors and textures. Treat yourself to helwa tat-Tork, a local sweet made from sugar, and nuts, and often flavored with rosewater or

citrus. These sweet temptations offer a glimpse into Malta's rich culinary heritage.

## 16. Local Beverages: Beyond Wine:

While Maltese wine is renowned, there are other local beverages worth exploring. Quench your thirst with a glass of the traditional prickly pear juice, made from the sweet and succulent fruit found on the island's cacti. It offers a refreshing and unique taste. If you prefer non-alcoholic options, try the Maltese soft drink Kinnie, a bittersweet carbonated beverage made from bitter oranges and aromatic herbs. These local beverages are perfect for staying hydrated and experiencing the unique flavors of Malta.

## 17. Sustainable and Farm-to-Table Experiences:

Malta's commitment to sustainability and supporting local farmers is reflected in its farm-to-table experiences. Embrace the farm-to-fork philosophy by dining at restaurants that prioritize locally sourced ingredients. Many establishments work directly with farmers, fishermen, and artisans to showcase the freshest produce and promote sustainable practices. Immerse yourself in the flavors of Malta while supporting the local economy and reducing your ecological footprint.

18. Recipe Inspiration and Cooking Tips:
To truly immerse yourself in Maltese cuisine, experiment with traditional recipes in your kitchen. Gather inspiration from the local dishes you've tasted and incorporate Maltese flavors into your cooking. Explore the unique combination of ingredients and experiment with the abundant seafood and local produce. Consider attending cooking classes or workshops to learn more about authentic techniques and secret family recipes. Let Maltese cuisine inspire your culinary creations and bring a taste of Malta to your home.

Maltese cuisine is a journey of flavors, traditions, and culinary heritage. From savory pastries to hearty stews, fresh seafood, and delightful desserts, each bite tells a story of the island's history and cultural influences. By exploring the local markets, participating in cooking classes, and savoring the diverse range of flavors, you will deepen your understanding of Maltese cuisine and create lasting memories. Allow your taste buds to guide you through this culinary adventure, and savor the rich tapestry of flavors that make Maltese cuisine truly exceptional.

19. Culinary Influences and Cultural Significance:
Maltese cuisine is a melting pot of culinary influences due to the island's strategic location and rich history. Explore the impact of Italian, North African, Arabic, and British cuisines on Maltese dishes. Discover how the spice trade introduced an array of flavors, herbs, and spices to the local

cuisine. Learn about the significance of food in Maltese culture, including the importance of communal dining, seasonal celebrations, and traditional family recipes passed down through generations.

20. Sustainability and Organic Farming:

As sustainability becomes increasingly important, Malta has embraced organic farming practices and sustainable food initiatives. Learn about organic farms, such as Ta' Mena and Abraham's, that prioritize environmental stewardship and produce high-quality organic ingredients. Discover restaurants that support sustainable fishing practices and source their ingredients from local suppliers. Engage with the farm-to-table movement in Malta, appreciating the efforts to protect the environment while enjoying delicious and nutritious meals.

21. Culinary Heritage and Historical Context:
Delve into the historical context of Maltese cuisine, understanding how the island's history has shaped its culinary traditions. Learn about the influence of the Phoenicians, Romans, Arabs, and Knights of St. John on the island's gastronomy. Explore the agricultural practices, fishing techniques, and cooking methods that have been passed down through generations. Gain a deeper appreciation for the cultural heritage embedded within the flavors of Maltese cuisine.

22. Experiencing Local Festivals and Celebrations:
Malta is known for its vibrant festivals and cultural celebrations, many of which revolve around food. Plan your visit to coincide with the Festa season, where each village celebrates its patron saint with elaborate processions, music, and, of course, feasting. Experience the colorful displays of

traditional sweets and pastries, such as prinjolata, during Carnival season. Immerse yourself in the festive atmosphere, enjoying the live music, traditional dances, and delectable food that showcase the joyous spirit of Malta.

23. Unique Food Souvenirs:
Bring a taste of Malta back home with you by seeking out unique food souvenirs. Explore local food markets and specialty shops to discover artisanal products like traditional honey, prickly pear jam, locally sourced sea salt, and infused olive oils. These authentic flavors will serve as a delicious reminder of your culinary journey through Malta and make for memorable gifts for friends and family.

24. Exploring Culinary Tours and Experiences:
Enhance your culinary adventure by joining guided culinary tours and experiences. Engage with knowledgeable guides who will

lead you through the vibrant food scene, highlighting hidden gems and local favorites. Take part in food and wine pairings, sample traditional dishes, and learn about the history and cultural significance of the foods you encounter. These tours provide an immersive and enriching experience, allowing you to fully appreciate the nuances and complexities of Maltese cuisine.

Maltese cuisine is a gateway to the island's rich history, cultural heritage, and culinary diversity. From traditional dishes to sustainable practices and vibrant festivals, each aspect of Maltese gastronomy tells a story. By exploring the influences, sustainability initiatives, and cultural context of the cuisine, you'll gain a deeper appreciation for the flavors and traditions of Malta. Embrace the joy of tasting local specialties, engaging with the community, and discovering the hidden culinary gems that make Malta a truly exceptional destination for food enthusiasts.

# Chapter 10

## Practical Information and Tips

In this of "Exploring Malta: The Ultimate Travel Guide to a Mediterranean Gem," we provide readers with essential practical information and valuable tips to ensure a smooth and enjoyable trip to Malta. From currency and language to accommodations and local customs, this chapter covers everything you need to know to make the most of your visit.

1. Essential Travel Information:
 - Currency: The official currency in Malta is the Euro (EUR). ATMs are widely available, and credit cards are widely accepted.
 - Language: The official languages are Maltese and English. English is spoken and understood by the majority of the population, making communication easy for English-speaking visitors.

- Safety: Malta is generally a safe destination for travelers. However, it's always wise to take common-sense precautions, such as being aware of your surroundings and keeping your belongings secure.

2. Accommodations:
    - Malta offers a wide range of accommodation options to suit every budget and preference. From luxurious resorts and boutique hotels to cozy guesthouses and self-catering apartments, there is something for everyone.
    - Popular areas to stay include Valletta, Sliema, St. Julian's, and Mellieha. Consider your preferred location, proximity to attractions, and access to public transportation when choosing your accommodation.

3. Getting Around:
    - Public Transportation: Malta has a reliable public bus network that covers most

areas of the islands. The bus service is an affordable and convenient way to get around. You can purchase a Tallinja card, which offers discounted fares.

- Taxis: Taxis are available throughout Malta. Ensure the taxi is licensed and metered or agree on a price before starting the journey.

- Car Rental: Renting a car provides flexibility and convenience for exploring Malta. Rental agencies are present at the airport and various locations across the islands. Remember to familiarize yourself with local driving rules and regulations.

4. Dining and Cuisine:

- Maltese cuisine is a delightful fusion of Mediterranean flavors influenced by Italian, North African, and Middle Eastern cuisines.

- Don't miss trying the national dish of Malta, rabbit stew (fenkata), which is rich and savory. Other local specialties include pastizzi (flaky pastries filled with cheese or peas), ftira (traditional Maltese bread), and hobz biz-zejt (a bread and tomato paste sandwich).

  - The islands are home to numerous restaurants, ranging from casual eateries serving traditional Maltese fare to fine dining establishments offering gourmet experiences.

5. Local Customs and Etiquette:

  - Religion: Malta is predominantly Catholic, and the locals hold their religious traditions in high regard. It is respectful to dress modestly when visiting churches or religious sites.

  - Greetings: When meeting someone for the first time, a handshake is the common greeting. Friends and acquaintances may exchange kisses on both cheeks.

  - Tipping: Tipping is appreciated in Malta. It is customary to leave a 10% tip for good service at restaurants, cafes, and bars. Hotel staff, taxi drivers, and tour guides also appreciate a small tip.

6. Useful Phrases:
   - While English is widely spoken, learning a few basic phrases in Maltese can enhance your interactions with the locals. Here are a few helpful phrases:
   - Hello: Bongu
   - Thank you: Grazzi
   - Yes: Iva
   - No: Le
   - Excuse me: Skużani
   - Goodbye: Saħħa

7. Safety and Health:
   - Medical Facilities: Malta has a well-developed healthcare system, and medical facilities are easily accessible. It is advisable to have travel insurance that covers any medical expenses during your stay.
   - Emergency Numbers: In case of emergencies, dial 112 for general emergencies or 196 for the police. Familiarize yourself with the nearest

hospital or medical center to your accommodation.

8. Weather and Best Time to Visit:

 - Malta enjoys a Mediterranean climate, with mild winters and hot summers. The best time to visit is during the spring (April to June) and autumn (September to October) when the weather is pleasant, and the crowds are thinner.

 - Springtime offers mild temperatures, blooming flowers, and fewer tourists. It's an excellent time for outdoor activities and exploring historical sites.

 - Autumn brings warm temperatures, making it ideal for beach visits and outdoor adventures. It's also the time when cultural events and festivals take place.

9. Travel Advisories and Requirements:

 - Before traveling to Malta, it's essential to check the latest travel advisories and entry requirements. This includes passport validity, visa requirements, and any specific COVID-19-related guidelines and protocols.

- Stay informed about any travel restrictions, quarantine measures, and testing requirements that may be in place during your planned visit.

10. Suggested Itineraries and Maps:

- To assist you in planning your time in Malta, we have included suggested itineraries and maps to help you navigate the islands efficiently.

- Detailed maps of Valletta, Mdina, Gozo, Comino, and other key areas highlight attractions, accommodations, transportation hubs, and suggested routes.

- Itineraries are provided for various durations, from short weekend trips to longer stays, ensuring you can make the most of your time on the islands.

11. Shopping and Souvenirs:

 - Malta offers a variety of shopping experiences, from bustling markets to modern shopping centers. Valletta and Sliema are popular areas for shopping, with a range of boutiques, designer stores, and local crafts.

 - Look out for unique souvenirs such as Maltese lace, filigree jewelry, traditional ceramics, and locally produced food products like honey and olive oil.

12. Communication and Connectivity:

 - Mobile Connectivity: Purchase a local SIM card or check with your mobile service provider for international roaming options to stay connected during your trip.

 - Wi-Fi: Most hotels, restaurants, and cafes offer free Wi-Fi. You can also find public Wi-Fi hotspots in various locations across the islands.

13. Cultural Etiquette:
   - Dress Code: While Malta is generally relaxed in terms of dress code, it is respectful to cover up when visiting religious sites or attending formal occasions.
   - Punctuality: Being punctual is appreciated in Malta, particularly for scheduled tours, events, or meetings.

14. Eco-Tourism and Responsible Travel:
   - Malta's natural beauty and fragile ecosystems make it important to practice responsible travel. Respect the environment, avoid littering, and follow designated paths during outdoor activities.
   - Support local businesses, artisans, and sustainable tourism initiatives to contribute positively to the local economy and community.

15. Hidden Gems and Off-the-Beaten-Path:
   - Discover lesser-known attractions and off-the-beaten-path destinations to experience the authentic charm of Malta.

Explore lesser-visited villages, coastal cliffs, and rural landscapes for a unique and tranquil experience.

16. Photography Tips:
   - Capture the beauty of Malta with these photography tips:
   - Golden Hour: Take advantage of the soft and warm light during sunrise and sunset for stunning photographs.
   - Architecture: Showcase the unique architectural details and colors of Malta's historical buildings.
   - Landscapes: Experiment with capturing the dramatic coastal cliffs, crystal-clear waters, and picturesque countryside.
   - Local Life: Capture candid shots of locals engaged in daily activities, capturing the essence of Maltese culture.

17. Travel Resources and Further Reading:
   - Provide a list of recommended travel resources, including websites, guidebooks, and blogs, where readers can find more

detailed information and insights about Malta.

With this comprehensive practical information and valuable tips, you are well-equipped to plan and enjoy an unforgettable trip to Malta. From navigating transportation to understanding local customs, embrace the rich culture, history, and natural beauty of this enchanting Mediterranean destination. Happy travels!

# Conclusion

Congratulations! You have reached the end of this comprehensive travel guide to Malta, a captivating Mediterranean gem that offers a unique blend of history, natural beauty, and vibrant culture. Throughout this book, we have explored the enchanting islands of Malta, Gozo, and Comino, delving into their rich heritage, must-visit attractions, outdoor adventures, culinary delights, and practical information to help you plan an unforgettable trip.

Malta, with its fascinating history dating back thousands of years, has a treasure trove of historical sites and architectural wonders. The capital city of Valletta, a UNESCO World Heritage site, boasts magnificent landmarks such as St. John's Co-Cathedral, with its awe-inspiring Baroque interior, and the Grandmaster's Palace, showcasing the opulence of the Knights of St. John. Exploring Valletta's narrow streets and charming squares, you'll uncover hidden gems and enjoy breathtaking views from the Upper Barrakka Gardens.

Venturing beyond Valletta, we discovered the ancient fortified city of Mdina, known as the "Silent City." Lose yourself in its medieval atmosphere, wander through its winding streets, and visit St. Paul's Cathedral and the fascinating Mdina Dungeons. Next, we explored the tranquil island of Gozo, where time seems to stand still. Marvel at the stunning Azure Window (formerly) and delve into the mysteries of the Ggantija Temples, among the oldest freestanding structures in the world. The picturesque village of Xlendi and the Citadel in Victoria are also not to be missed.

For relaxation and natural beautyContinuing our journey, we made our way to the idyllic island of Comino, home to the famous Blue Lagoon. Immerse yourself in the crystal-clear turquoise waters, soak up the sun on pristine beaches, and explore the island's secluded coves and walking trails. Comino offers a peaceful retreat where you can disconnect from the hustle and bustle of everyday life.

Malta is not just a destination for history and relaxation; it also offers a myriad of outdoor adventures. Dive into its underwater wonders, where vibrant marine life and fascinating shipwrecks await. Snorkel through azure waters, windsurf along the coast, or embark on exhilarating hikes and cycling trails, immersing yourself in Malta's stunning landscapes.

No visit to Malta would be complete without experiencing its delectable cuisine. Sample the flavors of the Mediterranean with a Maltese twist. Indulge in pastizzi, flaky pastries filled with ricotta or mushy peas, or savor traditional dishes like rabbit stew (fenkata) and fresh seafood caught daily. Be sure to visit local markets and restaurants, where you can taste the authentic flavors of Malta and engage in culinary adventures.

As you plan your trip to Malta, keep in mind the best time to visit. The spring months of April to June and the autumn months of September to October offer pleasant temperatures, fewer crowds, and the chance to witness traditional festivals and cultural events. However, Malta's mild winters and hot summers also have their charm, with unique celebrations and activities taking place throughout the year.

Throughout this guide, we have provided you with practical information to make your journey smooth and hassle-free. From visa requirements and transportation options to suggestions for accommodations and safety tips, we want to ensure you have all the necessary information at your fingertips.

Now, armed with this knowledge, it's time to embark on your adventure in Malta. Create lasting memories as you explore the historical treasures, soak up the natural beauty, indulge in the local flavors, and immerse yourself in the vibrant culture of this captivating Mediterranean destination.

May your journey be filled with awe-inspiring moments, unforgettable experiences, and a deep appreciation for the wonders that Malta has to offer. So pack your bags, embrace the spirit of adventure, and get ready to discover the magic of Malta!